CRY OUT
TO THE
Lord

BroadStreet Publishing Group, LLC
Racine, Wisconsin, USA
BroadStreetPublishing.com

CRY OUT TO THE *Lord*
O RESET *My Walk with God*

Cover by Chris Garborg at www.garborgdesign.com
Interior by Kimberly Sagmiller at www.fudgecreative.com

Printed in China
16 17 18 19 20 5 4 3 2 1

SPIRIT-
EMPOWERED
Faith

CRY OUT
TO THE
Lord

○ RESET

My Walk with God

BroadStreet
PUBLISHING

Contents

SECTION 1

SECTION 2

SECTION 3

Section 4

Section 5

Appendix:

Preface

Sometimes it's for you. Sometimes it's for a child, your family, or a friend. Sometimes it's for our nation or a broken world. We've all been there: we've all felt the need to *personally* cry out to the Lord.

- There are times we CRY OUT TO THE LORD because we don't know what to do. Our prayer to Him is a prayer of HUMILITY. Haven't there been times when you have prayed Jehoshaphat's prayer, "[Lord], we do not know what to do, but we are looking to you for help?" (2 Chronicles 20:12).

- There are times we CRY OUT TO THE LORD because we have messed up, chosen poorly, or gone against God's plan for our lives. With REPENTANCE, you may have restored your relationship with the Lord by asking Him to give you "clean hands and a pure heart" (Psalm 24:3-4, NASB).

- There are times when we CRY OUT TO THE LORD out of a desire to YIELD to His Lordship and hope for His Spirit to fill us and overflow through us (Ephesians 5:18).

- There are times when we CRY OUT TO THE LORD in INTERCESSION. Haven't there been times when you've poured out the burdens of your heart and carried the needs of others before Him, even when you didn't know exactly what to pray (Romans 8:26)?

- And certainly there are times when we CRY OUT TO THE LORD, asking Him to REENGAGE us in living out the Great Commission. Haven't there been moments of prayer where you've asked the Lord of the harvest to reignite your passion for the lost and send you out (Luke 10:2)?

Cry Out to the Lord is designed to bring a fresh experience to these moments when we all cry out to God. The goal of this resource is to help you move beyond seeking to simply know or obey God's truth and to move toward experiencing it. As we actually experience truth in our relationship with Jesus, He will lead us into a relational faith. It's only a relational faith that will reset our walk with God.

In order to fully illustrate what a relational faith includes, we have defined forty different Spirit-empowered outcomes (see Appendix). *Cry Out to the Lord* is written with a focus on five of these outcomes:

1. A Spirit-empowered faith consistently practices self-denial, fasting, and solitude rest.
2. A Spirit-empowered faith lives out a passionate longing for purity and to please Him in all things.
3. A Spirit-empowered faith yields to the Holy Spirit's fullness as life in the Spirit brings supernatural intimacy with the Lord, the manifestation of divine gifts, and the witness of the fruit of the Spirit.
4. A Spirit-empowered faith expresses disciplined, bold, and believing prayer.

5. A Spirit-empowered faith champions Jesus as the only hope of eternal life and abundant living.

Just as we have all felt the need to cry out to God in a personal way, a Spirit-empowered disciple of Jesus is also committed to corporate times of prayer to the Lord. "Gather the elders...and cry out to the Lord" (Joel 1:14, NASB).

In response to the spiritual wake-up call on September 11, 2001, the Awakening America Alliance has been faithfully urging Christ's followers to gather for Cry Out America prayer gatherings across the nation and to engage in an annual rhythm of prayer through the National Prayer Accord. This *Cry Out to the Lord* resource is designed to support these corporate gatherings where faith, civic, and community groups cry out to the Lord on behalf of our country. Additionally, the "Cry Out to the Lord Order of Worship" is a useful tool for pastors and church leaders who desire to host their own corporate prayer gatherings (see Appendix).

Imagine what could be different if thousands of churches, with millions of people gathered and with one voice cried out to the Lord in humility, repentance, yieldedness, intercession, and reengagement with the Great Commission! (Visit www.awakeningamerica.us for more information.)

 RESET

A PRAYER TO BRING HOPE

RESET YOUR WALK WITH GOD

When your computer or mobile device freezes, you know to hit the reset button. A reset restores the system to its original design. Hitting "reset" gives it a fresh start. So what happens when it's something in your life that feels frozen? Do you ever wish you could start over? Everyone feels that at times. And Jesus is the reset. Jesus restores you to your original design. He gives you a fresh start. That's what we hope this resource does for your prayer life. May it be a fresh start in your relationship with Jesus!

The *Cry Out to the Lord* resource is intended to serve the Reset Movement.

Reset is a work of anyone and everyone who wants to see Jesus bring hope to this generation and to this nation. Reset began as a prayer and dream of a young leader from North Dakota named Nick Hall, to see this generation unite around Jesus. The vision was never about one person or organization but a partnership around Jesus—and Jesus calls everyone.

Reset is not an organization. Reset is a prayer and a movement of people sharing the message of the hope Jesus brings when we pray it. The vision is not to facilitate a passive audience, but to catalyze an army of individuals who are actively praying to Jesus to reset their lives, their communities, and their cities—and actively seeking to live a life reset by Jesus. While there are organizations involved, the fuel of this movement is you.

The Reset Movement has identified four ways to start your reset. These four ingredients are the inspiration for calls to action that we have inserted into each of the writings by the authors in this resource.

 LEARN to Encounter Jesus

 PRAY and Experience Scripture

 SHARE with Others in Community

 LOVE Others in Community

The message of Reset is that Jesus can and will reset your life. And that same message and invitation is shared at Reset events. The events are a place to connect in person with others who are praying and living reset lives, hear stories of what Jesus is doing, and celebrate Jesus with hundreds and thousands of others who are praying for a reset. Go to www.resetmovement.com for more information.

Finally, The Great Commandment Network is thrilled to serve each contributor and ministry partner through this resource. Our resource development and training team serves various partners as they develop Spirit-empowered disciples who walk intimately with God's Son, God's Word, and God's people. May Jesus richly bless the unity, commitment, and faith that *Cry Out to the Lord* represents.

Terri Snead
Executive Editor, Great Commandment Network

The Great Commandment Network is an international collaborative network of strategic kingdom leaders from the faith community, marketplace, education, and caregiving fields who prioritize the powerful simplicity of the words of Jesus to love God, love others, and see others become His followers (Matthew 22:37–40, Matthew 28:19–20).

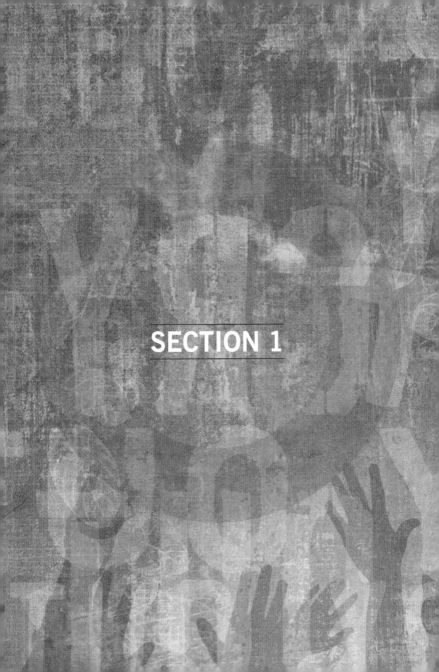

SECTION 1

I CHOOSE TO HUMBLE MYSELF AND SEEK HIS FACE

O LORD; attend to my cry!
Give ear to my prayer from lips free of deceit!
I call upon you, for you will answer me, O God;
incline your ear to me; hear my words.
Wondrously show your steadfast love....
Keep me as the apple of your eye;
hide me in the shadow of your wings.
(Psalm 17:1, 6–8 ESV)

A SPIRIT-EMPOWERED FAITH

consistently practices self-denial, fasting, and solitude. Let these authors encourage your Spirit-empowered faith:

- Ronnie Floyd—When Should You Call upon the Lord?
- Mark Williams—Teach Us to Pray
- Jeremy Story—Transformation through Prayer and Fasting
- Dennis Gallaher—Sabbath Rest

1

WHEN SHOULD YOU CALL UPON THE LORD?

From *How to Pray*
by Ronnie Floyd

CRY OUT TO THE LORD

Lord, my hope is not in more money, a different government, a new relationship, or a change of circumstance. My hope is in You and You alone. I humbly declare, "Your ways are not my ways, and Your thoughts are not my thoughts."

(Isaiah 55:8, paraphrased)

Help me to call upon You all the days of my life.

PREFACE

Scripture is clear that every Christian should practice calling upon the Lord in prayer. Like the psalmist David, we're encouraged to pray personally: "I cried out to the LORD; yes, I prayed to my God for help. He heard me from his sanctuary; my cry to him reached his ears" (Psalm 18:6). And Joel 1:14 reminds us to pray corporately: "Bring the leaders and all the people of the land into the Temple of the LORD your God, and cry out to him there." When should believers call upon the Lord? Here are five situations in which Christians should call upon the Lord.

Call upon the Lord All the Time

Do you call upon the Lord all the time or only when you need something? Do you call upon Him out of conviction or out of crisis? Is your life organized enough so that you can spend time daily time with Him in prayer? Do you have a plan that allows time for you to call upon the Lord in prayer? Your spiritual life should not have to be in an intensive care unit for you to pray. Calling upon the Lord continually demonstrates that we are depending upon the Lord rather than ourselves. Call upon the Lord all the time, every day.

Call upon the Lord in a Time of Need

Just as parents love for their children to call on them in a time of need, God loves for His children to do the same. Calling upon the Lord in a time of need does not indicate a lack of faith, but an understanding that God is the ultimate object of our faith. God can do anything, anywhere, and at any time. He can provide for your need.

What kind of need do you have today? I do not believe God categorizes our needs as big or small. At times, we may be tempted to handle the small things and let God handle just the big things. It is as if we are saying "God, we know You are so busy that we will bother You with just the things that we know we cannot handle by ourselves." Prayerlessness indicates dependence upon ourselves. This attitude is wrong. God wants us to come to Him in prayer about all of our needs.

What is your need today? Do you need healing? All healing takes place because of God. Do you need money? Honor Him with what you have, and He will provide for your need. Do you have a relationship that is strained? Only God can bring two hostile or

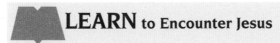

opposing persons together. Do you have a material need? Call upon the Lord! He is able to meet even your material needs.

I believe that God creates needs in your life for the purpose of causing you to depend upon Him. He wants you to rely upon Him. He wants to do the impossible. He loves to show others that with Him all things are possible. Even before your need exists, God already has the supply.

LEARN to Encounter Jesus

He always lives to make intercession for [you]. (Hebrews 7:25, NASB)

Imagine that you walk into a room and find Jesus engaged in prayer. You may not hear the specific words He is using, but you are confident that Christ is praying for someone He dearly loves. You peer over Jesus' shoulder and, to your surprise, your own prayer list is lying in front of Him. Jesus is praying for you—the Savior is praying for *your* needs, *your* temptations, and *your* heartfelt struggles. He is praying for the very vision, ministry, and calling that you hope to pursue.

How does it make you feel to know that Jesus intercedes on your behalf? He spends time talking to His Father about you—not judging you or condemning you, not in criticism or in ridicule. Jesus speaks to the Father and reminds Him of your needs, and He reminds Him of the price He paid on the cross so that you might have abundant life both now and forever. How does it make you feel to reflect on Jesus' prayers for you?

As I reflect on how Jesus prays for me, I am filled with _____gratitude_____ .

Finally, consider the reality that Jesus often prays to the Father about your needs, but He does so without you. Jesus prays alone. Is there something in your spirit that is prompted to join Him more often? Tell Jesus about that now.

Jesus, as I imagine You interceding for me—often without me— I feel _____.

I want You to hear the feelings of my heart concerning _____.

I am so grateful for You _____.

CALL UPON THE LORD IN A TIME OF PURSUING THE FUTURE

Some of the most important decisions you will make in life have to do with planning your future. When pursuing what lies ahead, call upon the Lord. He is able to give to you guidance and wisdom in regard to your future. The Bible promises you a great life, wonderful welfare, and God's peace as you call upon the Lord in prayer (see Jeremiah 29:11).

One of the pivotal questions each person must ask pertaining to his or her future is, *God, what do You want me to do?* My life is not my own; I belong to God. I am not owned by any man or any system. I am not the property of this world. I am God's property. Since He owns the title to my life, I must take directions pertaining to my future from Him.

CALL UPON THE LORD IN A TIME OF WORSHIP

In moments of public worship, are you calling upon the Lord? Is your day for worship set aside for the purpose of worshipping Him? Before you go to worship at your church, talk to God. Summon Him to meet with you and the entire body of Christ that is sharing the experience with you.

Much of the worship in church life today is stale and power-less. As a result, lives are left unchanged. Could this be happening because we do not spend time calling upon the Lord in worship? Much of worship today centers on personalities and performance, rather than the Lord and His work in the lives of people. Worship should never be about the people in attendance. Worship should exalt the Lord Jesus and be focused on calling upon Him in prayer. Call upon the Lord in a time of worship.

 ## PRAY and Experience Scripture

God decided in advance to adopt us into his own family by bringing us to himself through Jesus Christ. This is what he wanted to do, and it gave him great pleasure. So we praise God for the glorious grace he has poured out on us…. (Ephesians 1:5–6)

Take a few moments to consider the incredible truth that you have been brought into a relationship with the One of whom all these things are true. How does it make you feel to realize that you have the privilege to know, love, and be loved by such a Savior? What does it do to your heart to imagine that God smiles with pleasure when He thinks about you being a part of His family? Take a few moments to praise Him now for His gracious gift found in Christ Jesus.

Lord Jesus, as I think about the incredible privilege of having a relationship with You, my heart is filled with _____.
(For example, *gratitude, love, joy, praise, a sense of unworthiness, peace, awe,* or *wonder.*)

I feel _____ *when I imagine Your smile, because I'm a part of Your family. I praise You for loving me.*

CALL UPON THE LORD IN A DESIGNATED PRAYER TIME

Do you have a designated time of prayer in your life? Make a date with God daily. Find a plan to follow. First things first! Get alone with God at the first of the day. Use this time to call upon the Lord in prayer. Let it be the time every day when you bare your heart to God about your life and your greatest needs. Take the time to listen to what He says to you after you share your heart with Him.

A final important suggestion: Make an appeal to the pastors and leaders in your church to set aside worship services that are dedicated solely to prayer. God can do more in a moment of prayer than in all the programs one church could do in a lifetime. Determine to make your church a praying church. Decide today, how you can walk alongside your pastor, helping him create a fellowship of believers who practice calling upon the Lord in prayer. Stand up and be different. Be a Christian who calls upon the Lord in prayer.

 SHARE with Others in Community

Everyone who is fully trained will be like their teacher. (Luke 6:40, NIV)

Imagine Christ standing before you—the only true Teacher (Matthew 23:10), and the One who lives to make intercession for you (Hebrews 7:25). Your Teacher loves to pray; in fact, He lives to pray. Reflect on your opportunity to pray with Jesus. Then talk to a friend, family member, or mentor about your willingness and desire to become a person of prayer, just like your Teacher. Invite this person to pray with you on a regular basis.

➡️ LOVE Others in Community

Pause quietly to consider this question: Lord, *who needs me to pray for them and call upon You to help them?*

    Lord, I call out to You on behalf of _____.

    You know the needs, and I'm asking You to _____.

    By faith, I am claiming the promise that _____.

    How can I show Your love to this person?

2

TEACH US TO PRAY

From *The Praying Church Handbook*, Volume II
by Mark Williams

CRY OUT TO THE LORD

Lord, I cry out to You today. Help me to be still and listen to You. Open my eyes to see You more clearly. Open my ears to hear Your voice and then sense the things that are on Your heart. Help me make the things of God my priority. I pray with many Christians throughout the ages:
Lord, teach me to pray.

PREFACE

Prayer is our simple but amazing privilege to communicate with the Lord, experiencing unhindered intimacy and fellowship with Him. Through prayer we boldly go into the throne room of the Almighty, the very dwelling place of the Most High. God loves our prayers—He loves to hear us talk to Him and He loves to show Himself mighty in answering what we ask of Him. In fact, the book of Revelation tells us that our prayers are like sweet perfume to the Lord—the fragrance of our worshipful hearts sweetens the presence of God (Revelation 5:8). How amazing would it be and how pleased would God be if every Christ-follower became a person of intimate prayer?

The one quality that seems to most characterize the life of Jesus Christ and makes the deepest impact upon His disciples was His prayer life. Jesus Christ was a man of prayer. Sure, He raised the dead. Sure, He brought sight to the blind. Sure, He made the lame to walk and the blind to see—but none of this was accomplished without prayer. Prayer was the driving force of His ministry. It was the energizing force of His life. Prayer was the passion of His very existence. When He walked into the temple and found those who were buying and selling oxen, sheep, and doves, others who were making merchandise of the gospel, He became enraged and overthrew the tables of the money changers, and the seats of them that sold doves, took a chord and drove them out of the temple, and said, "It is written, 'My house shall be called the house of prayer; but ye have made it a den of thieves'" (Matthew 21:13). He believed in prayer so strongly that He "spoke a parable unto them to this end, that men ought always to pray, and not to faint" (Luke 18:1).

Jesus practiced what He preached. Time and again, the Scripture reveals Jesus making prayer a priority. At all times and in all ways, Jesus prayed. Jesus prayed for Himself. Jesus prayed for His disciples! Jesus prayed for all who would believe on Him! Jesus prayed frequently! Jesus prayed faithfully! Jesus prayed fervently! Jesus prayed fruitfully!

Most importantly, right now, Jesus is praying for you! He is the great High Priest, and He ever lives to make intercession for us!

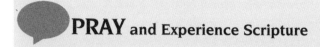

PRAY and Experience Scripture

Give thanks to the LORD and proclaim his greatness. (1 Chronicles 16:8)

Jesus was a model for us because He prayed for specific people. In fact, when Jesus told Peter that he was going to experience persecution, Jesus actually told him that he made the Savior's prayer list. Luke reminds us, "Jesus said to Peter, 'But I have prayed for you'" (Luke 22:32). But what's more amazing is that Christ doesn't just pray for Peter or for people who lived in the first century; He prays for you too. Isn't it amazing to know that we have a historical Jesus, but we also have a contemporary Jesus? This is why the writer of Hebrews says that He is the "same yesterday, today, and forever" (Hebrews 13:8).

Pause quietly to picture Jesus bowed in prayer. When Christ finishes His prayer, He lifts His head and says the same to you: "Dear one, I have prayed for you." He then begins to tell you about the prayers of protection that He is praying for your life, the prayers of provision and the divine intervention He has asked for on your behalf. Jesus explains all that He is sharing with the Father because He deeply cares for you. Now respond to Him in gratitude. Give Him thanks and declare His greatness.

Thank You, Lord, for being a present-tense, right-now Jesus. I'm grateful that You are praying for me because _____. *You are great because* _____.

Secondly, for prayer to be effective, Jesus says that we must remember that prayer is based on relationship. That intimate union between a believer and his Lord, whereby we see God, not as some sovereign dictate of heaven that is void of love and compassion, not as the Unmoved Mover, but we come to understand that God is, "Our Father which art in heaven." We must come to recognize that God is transcendent, but He is also immanent. He is the high and lofty One who inhabits eternity, but He is also a very present help in the time of need. And Jesus, the one who prays for us, is both fully God and fully human. We have the opportunity to relate to someone who is as real and human as our next door neighbor and at the same time, a sovereign and omnipotent King. And just as Scripture notes that Abraham was a "friend of God," we can rejoice that we also are a friend of God. He reveals Himself to you and involves you in prayerful intimacy!

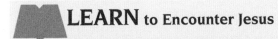

LEARN to Encounter Jesus

Reflect on Christ's final moments in the garden of Gethsemane. The divinity of our Savior knew His sacrifice was going to be offered for our redemption. However, at the same time, the humanity of our Savior knew the pain He faced at Calvary would be unlike any pain He had ever known before. And out of that mixture of emotion, Jesus asked His disciples for support: "[Jesus] told them, 'My soul is crushed with grief to the point of death. Stay here and keep watch with me'" (Matthew 26:38).

Remarkably, at the saddest hour of Christ's earthly ministry, the time when the disciples where supposed to be awake and supportive of Jesus' upcoming sufferings, the disciples fell asleep. Even after Jesus repeatedly pled for them to join Him in prayer, His closest friends failed to pray. Remember Christ's pain-filled words at this point: "My soul is crushed with grief to the point of death. Stay here and keep watch with me…. Couldn't you watch with me even one hour?" (Matthew 26:38, 40).

Reflect on this scene for a moment. How might you have responded to Jesus' request to watch with Him? Is there something within you that longs to make up for what the disciples missed? Listen as the Holy Spirit speaks these same words to your heart: "Can you come pray with Me for just one hour?"

Respond to Jesus now.

As I *sense Your invitation for me to join You in prayer, my heart is moved to* _____.

Now celebrate! Through the blood of Jesus at Calvary, we who were once alienated and distanced from Him have been brought nigh and made to be part of the family of God! "For ye have not received the spirit of bondage again to fear; but ye have received the Spirit of adoption, whereby we cry, Abba, Father. The Spirit itself beareth witness with our spirit, that we are the children of God" (Romans 8:15, 16). We are heirs of God and joint heirs with Jesus Christ! Jesus is our elder brother and God is our Father! He is a Father who is dependable! He is a Father who loves, cares, and protects His own! He is Father to the fatherless! He is the Father who knows what we need before we ask Him! And if we, being earthly, "know how to give good gifts unto our children, how much more shall the heavenly Father give good gifts unto them that ask Him!" What a privilege to come into His presence and say, "Our Father which art in heaven!"

 SHARE with Others in Community

The decision Christ made in the garden and His choice to give His life at Calvary was the greatest demonstration of love we'll ever know. Jesus made the choice to give of His life at Calvary because He loved you so much that He wanted to give His life for you: "There is no greater love than to lay down one's life for one's friends" (John 15:13).

As His grateful ambassadors, we are called to pass on this divinely extravagant love. Some of Christ's final words on earth confirm this truth: "So now I am giving you a new commandment: Love each other. Just as I have loved you, you should love each other. Your love for one another will prove to the world that you are my disciples" (John 13:34–35). Refresh your commitment to this commandment. And pray this prayer with another Jesus-follower:

Father, I want to make You my priority as I live out the commandment You have for me. As I reflect on the privilege—and the wonder—of passing along the love You demonstrated, my heart is moved with _____. *Continue to reveal Yourself to me as I share Your love with those around me.*

➡ LOVE others in Community

I pray that the eyes of your heart may be enlightened, so that you will know what is the hope of His calling....(Ephesians 1:18, NASB)

Pray and ask God to open the eyes of your heart; ask Him to reveal the person or persons who need a fresh demonstration of Christ's love—through you. Claim the promise of Ephesians 1:18, that you might "see and hear," just as Jesus does.

Lord, open my eyes to the people You want me to love. Show me the person who needs a fresh demonstration of Your care this week. Reveal how You want me to be a part of loving them. Show me, Lord. I'm ready to demonstrate Your love in a real and life-giving way.

3

TRANSFORMATION THROUGH PRAYER AND FASTING

by Jeremy Story

CRY OUT TO THE LORD

Lord, I cry out to You and acknowledge that You are the Lord of my life. You are all-powerful over this world, and You are all-powerful over my heart. Empower me to live a life of faith in You. Make my life marked by fasting and prayer so that I am sensitive to Your Spirit and pleasing to You. God, I'm desperate for Your presence. I need You.

PREFACE

Our humility before the Lord is the beginning of great things that He is about to do in our lives. It is then our submission to His agenda and His power that paves the way for the Spirit's transformation, causing us to be more and more like Christ. We'll know true inner transformation has begun in our own lives and in our communities when one unified voice resonates with His love.

Recently I returned from the New York City area after living there for six years. During my time there I was reminded again how God lays out clear principles in the Bible to see any family, campus, city, or nation transformed.

New York and New England are known for being the toughest ground for ministry among us college students. However, during my time in New York City, we saw God do miraculous things. Thousands of students across the Northeast were mobilized into prayer and action. Together with other leaders, a city-wide prayer gathering was established, involving students from over fifty campuses. God united campus ministers in prayer and in plans for action across the city. This unified effort provided an environment where many college-focused churches and ministries were able to do things they had only dreamed of before.

Please don't misunderstand, there is still much more to do in New York City. The Bible promises us that this side of heaven there will always be more ways we need to see God's transformation. Would you like to know how to take transformation steps in your sphere of influence? Read on.

THE EPHESIAN ELEMENTS

Transforming a campus, business, or city may be a big topic, but the Bible does break it down into key elements. The Oxford Online Dictionary defines an "element" as, "A part or aspect of something abstract, especially one that is essential or characteristic." Paul's letter to the Ephesian church provides a clear outline of these essential elements.

ELEMENT 1: GOD'S ULTIMATE WILL IS TO SEE EVERYTHING SUBMITTED TO JESUS

The Bible actually tells us this clearly! Ephesians 1:9–10 (NIV) states, "He [God] made known to us the mystery of his will according-ing to his good pleasure, which he purposed in Christ, to be put into effect when the times reach their fulfillment—to bring unity to all things in heaven and on earth under Christ."

God is certainly moving now (as he has been since the first day of earthly history) to do one primary thing: Unite everything under the authority of Jesus. He created you, specifically to be a part of this plan. This means that every time you submit and obey God, even when the prevailing culture isn't, you are moving with the overall, forceful flow of history rather than against it. Don't shrink back because you have a hard time believing God's stated goal. Don't recoil because you think it's impossible for Jesus to reign in the lives of those around you. Let God's voice speak louder than the culture of your neighborhood, business, or city.

PRAY and Experience Scripture

God has now revealed to us his mysterious plan regarding Christ, a plan to fulfill his own good pleasure. And this is the plan: At the right time he will bring everything together under the authority of Christ—everything in heaven and on earth. (Ephesians 1:9–10)

Pause now and pray a prayer to the Lord, asking Him to continue to reveal the things in your life that need to be placed under His authority. Ask the Holy Spirit to reveal these things to your heart, in order to fulfill His good pleasure and purpose in your life.

Lord, what parts of my life need to be more pleasing to You? I want You to reveal any thought, action, attitude, or behavior that needs to be placed under Your authority. I submit to You, Lord. Forgive me for not allowing You to be Lord over every part of my life. I submit to You now and confess that Jesus is Lord.

After the Lord has spoken about the areas you need to submit to Him, consider including a regular day of fasting and prayer as a part of your submission to His plan.

ELEMENT 2: THE POWER OF JESUS IN YOU HAS AUTHORITY TO OVERCOME ANYTHING

By God's grace, not our virtue, Jesus' authority reigns in and through us now. Ephesians 1:21–23 (NIV) reminds us, "…He [God] raised Christ from the dead and seated him at his right hand in the heavenly realms, far above all rule and authority, power and dominion, and every name that is invoked, not only in the present age but also in the one to come. And God placed all things under his feet and appointed him to be head over everything for the church, which is his body, the fullness of him who fills everything in every way."

Don't accept that the things which are contrary to God's desires are unchangeable. God has placed us into his family, the body of Christ. God has placed "all rule and authority, power and dominion…under his feet," and because we are the body that authority is under our feet as well. Let us not be people who embrace the reality of God, but deny his every-day power in and through our lives. God wants you to live in purity and exercise his authority in prayer. He wants to dispel the darkness that brings bondage to our lives and the people around us.

Jesus, and the early Christ-followers, didn't beg God to act. They prayed with confidence that God *would* act. They knew God's authority could be directly appropriated through their prayers and resulting faith-filled actions. Ephesians 3:10 even tells us that the wisdom of God is revealed to beings in the heavenly realms through our actions here on earth!

LEARN to Encounter Jesus

Imagine the scene described in Ephesians. Christ is seated at the right hand of God in the heavenly realms. Imagine yourself kneeling before the One who has all things placed under His feet; He has been appointed the head over everything in the world. Picture the King on His throne, and as you sit at His feet He begins to remind you of where you are. You have the ability to talk and relate to the One who has the power to do anything He wants, the One who has the ability to change everything with just one word.

Picture the face of Jesus as He says to you, "Dear one, I am both the God of all comfort and the Lord God Almighty. I am the God of grace *and* I'm the Lord of all. It may seem difficult to imagine, but I can't wait for you to call upon Me and trust Me. Your faith actually brings Me pleasure. In fact, without faith it's impossible to please Me."

Spend a few moments meditating on this fact. In what area of your life do you need to trust Him more? In what new way can you depend upon Him and, by faith, wait for Him to act on your behalf?

Lord, in what area of my life do You want me to trust You more? Because You are the God of all grace, I know You care about me deeply. Thank You for Your fatherly care for me. And because You are the God of all power and dominion, the One who is seated at the Father's right hand, I trust You to work Your plans and purposes in my life.

After the Lord has spoken to you, consider including a regular day of fasting and prayer to sensitize your heart and empower your faith in what only God can do.

ELEMENT 3: UNITE WITH OTHER BELIEVERS TO MAGNIFY JESUS

Unity in prayer and action is the paramount hallmark of transformation. Ephesians 4:3 implores every believer to, "make every effort to keep the unity of the Spirit through the bond of peace." Outside of God's love for us, there is no greater recurring theme in the New Testament than the call to unite with other Christ-followers. Biblical unity doesn't mean uniformity. Ephesians 4:11 tells us that each of us are gifted in different and unique ways. We should fulfill our different callings and exercise our different gifts, but we should make every effort to bring together our different strengths. In fact, our differences were put there by God in order to reveal that we need each other and in the beauty of unity we see him more clearly.

Biblical unity also is a testament to the existence and relevance of Jesus. Ephesians 4:14 says that our oneness will actually better proclaim truth rather than water it down. When different people stand together around the same Christ; we speak more loudly into the culture around us.

SHARE with Others in Community

Ask a friend to share a specific prayer request or need with you and then vulnerably share your own with them. Spend some time praying over one another. Submit to the Lord's agenda for your prayer partner. Declare God's power over their life and then unite in prayer.

Lord, we are praying for _____, and we submit to Your plans and desires for this situation. We know that You are powerful enough to _____. And so, in unity we ask You by faith to _____.

LOVE Others in Community

Join with some friends in praying for God to involve each of you in changing your community. Unite in prayer and in action. Discuss and plan ways to express Christ's love to the people around you. Utilize your differing gifts, talents, and callings to collectively show God's love to those you come into contact with. Pray toward this plan in unity and with faith.

God, we want to be a picture of You in our community. How is the best way to show Your love? God, we know You promised to be with us when we gather together in Your name, so we trust you to_____. And we ask You in faith to involve us in showing love to our community by _____.

Finally, ask the Lord to give you an opportunity to tell an unchurched friend about the difference prayer is making in your life.

4

SABBATH REST

From A *Sabbath Rest*
by Dennis Gallaher

CRY OUT TO THE LORD

Lord, I don't want to live my life filled with stress, anxiety, or worry. I don't want my relationship with You to be all about rules to follow or things to avoid. I want to rest in the closeness of our relationship with one another. You promised rest to Your people. I'm claiming that promise for my life today. I rest in You, for You are my rest.

PREFACE

There has never been a time like the one in which we now live. There has never been more wealth and more leisure, but there has also never been more depression, suicide, and self-destruction. Could the two be linked together in some unseen diabolical plan? Or could it be that God's plan is for His saints to come to know such divine rest in the midst of the world's harsh realities, that they are able to reveal Him to the world around them? Perhaps God desires for us to exhibit such a restful spirit that others come to rest in Him as well. Whatever the case, we know that there is a rest for the people of God, and we are to do our best to enter into that rest (Hebrews 4:10–11).

Because of His Grace

"…God, who cannot lie, promised…so there remains a Sabbath rest for the people of God." (Titus 1:2; Hebrews 4:9 NIV)

Are you tired of the struggle? Do you look about and suppose that the God who loves you has chosen to bless others with good gifts and you only with pain?

Fear not, you're in good company. Not one person who is cataloged by faith in the Bible had an easy life. Instead, we read about lives that were marked by struggle, loss, pain and failure yet their stories are punctuated with this exclamation, "But God!" The litany of these faithful men and women reads like a tragic tale of loss, until God intervenes and shows Himself strong, turning trials into triumphs.

God has promised you rest and He cannot lie. Though you are bruised by the cold stones that catch your feet on what seems an endless trek, *God has promised rest and cannot lie*. Though you lie down in tears and hear only the lies of the evil one telling you that life will never change, *God has promised rest and cannot lie*. Every step you take is closer to His glory, so keep your eyes focused ahead and remember, *God has promised and cannot lie*!

Whatever path you are on is the path today ordered by the Lord. Phillips Brooks said,

Faith says not, "I see that it is good for me, so God must have sent it," but, "God sent it, and so it must be good for me."

There is a choice in rest. Do I choose to rest in God's ultimate plan and provision or strive to get beyond the Master's release? Choose well, friend. Choose to trust in God.

PRAY and Experience Scripture

What sorrow awaits those who argue with their Creator? (Isaiah 45:9)

Consider some of the recent circumstances that God has sent your way. Are you making the choice to rest in them, or are you quarreling or arguing with God about them? The prophet Isaiah reminds us that quarreling with our Creator will only bring us sorrow. But if quarreling with the Creator only brings sorrow, then how should we respond? We can gain insight into this question by looking at how Jesus responded to the Father in the midst of His pain and suffering. Jesus' response was to *yield*. His commitment to yield was so strong that He described it as His very nourishment: "'My food,' said Jesus, 'is to do the will of him who sent me and to finish his work'" (John 4:34, NIV).

One of the ways we can express our love to the Father is to yield to His will and to His ways for our life. Great love is expressed when we yield ourselves to the Creator of all things—even before we know His plan for us. One of the simplest ways to love God is to say, "Yes, Lord, now what would You have me do?"

Spend some time expressing your yielded heart to the Lord. Declare that the quarreling is over.

Lord, I acknowledge Your work in my life and I yield to it. Continue Your Spirit's work in me so that I would never again quarrel with You over what is best for my life. I trust that what You are doing is according to Your perfect plan for me. Help me to trust You when I doubt, Lord. Help me to trust You in the midst of the pain.

The Problem with Religion

"For the Son of Man is Lord, even over the Sabbath" (Matthew 12:8).

The Sabbath was what definitively separated the Jew from every other people group. It was not just a break in the week or a day off. It was an invitation from God to be separated totally for Him. Yahweh would provide. Yahweh would strengthen and bless. Yahweh would take thought of His people as His people took thought of Him. Other religions had temples, ceremonies, even circumcision, but no other religion had Sabbath as a seal of separation to their God.

Religion falsely promises that our efforts and rules will provide for us. That is why the Pharisees were so condemning of the behavior of the disciples. And that is why Jesus' words forever altered the relationship between the Sabbath and man. No longer would men earn their "moral keep" by obeying certain rules. Having a relationship with the Lord of the Sabbath would win the day.

LEARN to Encounter Jesus

Now I am coming to you. I told them many things while I was with them in this world so they would be filled with my joy. (John 17:13)

Recall Jesus' high priestly prayer, where Christ prays not only for the eleven remaining disciples but also for you and for me. One of His many requests in this prayer is that we would be filled with His joy. This is His will for you and me—that we might move away from religious thinking to a joy-filled, intimate relationship with God. We no longer have to question God's will for our lives. He has revealed it—that we may be filled with His joy.

It is time to respond to the Lord; it is time to yield to the fullness of this joy being expressed in your heart. Share your heart's desire to yield to what God is revealing to you, and to do so joyfully, with an eagerness to please Him.

Lord Jesus, I desire for Your joy to be made full in me. I want my nourishment to be obedience to all You reveal to me, which is motivated by the amazing privilege of entering into Your rest. May Your Spirit in me motivate me and empower me to please You in all things with my life. Let Your joy be made full within me.

THE NEVER ENDING DAY

"…And God blessed the seventh day and declared it holy, because it was the day when he rested from all his work of creation" (Genesis 2:3).

It is a common thought, so old that it has earned the title of tradition. The Jewish sages noted it first in their writings about the Sabbath and many have written of it since. It is this: Each of the six days of creation ends with the finality of "it was evening and the morning." The Jewish day would begin at sunset and end when three stars were visible the following twilight. It began in darkness and ended in darkness, the day caught between the bookends of night.

But the seventh day was different. The final day, God's day of rest, began but did not end as the other days. The Scriptures separate it from the other days by the word "sanctify"—which means to set apart for a special purpose. The purpose of that seventh day was that God rested from all His works. All of creation was finished. All that was created was "very good." According to the sages, the day was never meant to end.

The writer of Hebrews said, "So there remains a Sabbath rest for the people of God" (Hebrews 4:9 NASB).

Spoken to the church, it was a promise that beyond salvation was a life to be attained that looked more like the garden than the world in which we live. It is the life of Sabbath, a continual trust in the provision of God that breaths out the peace of God and inhales back His mercies. Sabbath is not a day or an event: it is a lifestyle promised, yet only obtained if we choose to enter in.

And you are invited. Sabbath awaits you today…or tonight… or this afternoon or weekend. Because God's plan was for His children to always know His rest, even in the midst of this tribulation we call life.

 # SHARE with others in Community

Talk to a friend, family member, or mentor about your desire for more of God's Sabbath rest. Spend some intentional moments in quiet prayer and reflection together. Cry out to the Lord and ask Him to show you the places of your life where He wants to bring more of His peace. Spend time talking about practical ways to intentionally build more rest into your days, weeks, months, and years.

 # LOVE Others in Community

Ask God to show you a person or persons who could benefit from more of God's Sabbath rest. Then ask Him to reveal specific ways that you might show this person some of God's provision, His hope, and His peace.

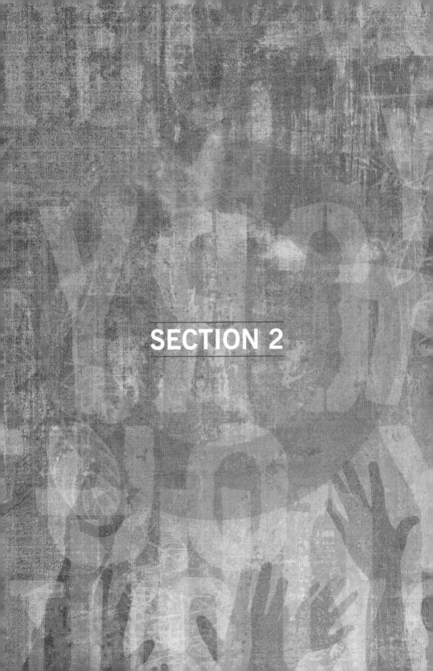

SECTION 2

I WILL TURN FROM MY SIN AND SELF-EFFORT

Out of the depths I cry to you, O Lord!
O Lord, hear my voice!
Let your ears be attentive to the
voice of my pleas for mercy!
If you, O Lord, should mark my iniquities,
O Lord, who could stand?
But with you there is forgiveness,
that you may be feared.
(Psalm 130:1–4 ESV)

A SPIRIT-EMPOWERED FAITH

lives out a passionate longing for purity and to please God in all things. Let these authors encourage your Spirit-empowered faith:

- Dave Butts—A Proper Reaction to Personal Sin
- Doug Beacham—On Our Knees
- David Ferguson—Godly Sorrow: Key to Repentance
- Byron Paulus and Bill Elliff—Revival Reality

5

A PROPER REACTION TO PERSONAL SIN

From *When God Shows Up*
by Dave Butts

CRY OUT TO THE LORD

Lord, I want to be honest with You about my sin. I want to turn away from sinfulness, ask for Your forgiveness, and because of that forgiveness revel in the closeness of the relationship I have with You. I want the times of refreshing that You have promised: "Repent, then, and turn to God, so that your sins may be wiped out, that times of refreshing may come from the Lord."
(Acts 3:19 NIV)

PREFACE

As followers of Jesus pray for revival, most of us understand, at least at some level, that our own sin indicates the need for revival and that our sin may also be blocking the coming of that revival. Looking to past revivals for guidance, it seems that without repentance there is no expectation of revival. Therefore, it becomes imperative that we demonstrate a proper response to personal sin. As we get serious about dealing with our own sin, then God begins to respond to our prayers and pleas for His presence, demonstrating His power by awakening our hearts and the hearts of others.

Dealing with personal sin is something that should be taught at an early stage in our Christian life. The apostle John tells us, "If we claim to be without sin, we deceive ourselves" (1 John 1:8 NIV). How do Christians deal with personal sin in an intentional way so that we are not deceived? There appear to be two extremes that many believers struggle with. One extreme that seems prevalent in the church today is to ignore sin, or to distort its seriousness. We lose sight of the call to holiness and what it means to follow Jesus. The other extreme is to be afraid that every time you sin you've lost your salvation. There are those who live in such a state of fear that they can hardly function as Christians.

The biblical way to deal with personal sin is perhaps best found in Psalm 51. David wrote and prayed this psalm right after he had been exposed as an adulterer and murderer. We can learn the proper reaction to personal sin from David.

First, there must be an acknowledgement of sin. Until we accept the fact that there is sin in our lives, there can be no confession, forgiveness, or restoration. Confession is basically agreeing with God that what we have done is sin. In Psalm 51:4, David makes the important step of realizing that sin is an affront to God Himself: "Against you, you only, have I sinned and done what is evil in your sight." When we understand this fact, sorrow for our sin becomes real and leads to further steps.

As David begins to understand the depths of his sin, he expresses his desire for cleansing and forgiveness. In his eagerness to receive forgiveness, he uses a variety of terms: "have mercy," "blot out," "wash away," "cleanse." It all comes down to asking God for forgiveness. The promise of Scripture is that God will forgive. It is important for Christians to memorize and believe with all their hearts the truth of 1 John 1:9: "If we confess our sins, he is faithful and just and will forgive us our sins and purify us from all unrighteousness."

 PRAY and Experience Scripture

Have mercy on me, O God, because of your unfailing love. Because of your great compassion, blot out the stain of my sins. Wash me clean from my guilt. Purify me from my sin. (Psalm 51:1–2)

Be still before the Lord and offer the same type of prayers that David prayed as he repented of his sin.

*Search me, O Lord, for **sins that hinder me** from hearing You. Free me from all moral filth, evil, malice, deceit, hypocrisy, envy, and slander. Free me to have a cleansed heart and mind. Speak now, Lord, for I am listening.*

*Search me, O Lord, for **unresolved emotions** that keep me from hearing You. Free me from any guilt or condemnation, any anger or bitterness, any fear or anxiety. Free me to live each moment in the present with You.*

*Search me, O Lord, for **childish things** that distract me from hearing You. Free me from rationalizing my behavior and blaming others. Free me to practice personal responsibility before You and others.*

*Search me, O Lord, for areas of **self-focus** that prevent me from hearing You. Free me from my thoughts, my ways, my ideas, and my goals. May I instead embrace Your thoughts, Your ways, Your ideas, and Your goals. Speak now, Lord, for I am listening.*

Wait before the Lord. Listen as He reveals what needs to be put away from your life.

Lord, I sense the need to put away _____
from my life. I ask Your forgiveness for holding onto this. Remove it from
my life so that I can draw closer to You.

True repentance never stays merely at the stage of confessing sin and desiring forgiveness. It moves us beyond that to a desire for a pure heart. There comes a longing to stay out of sin and to walk in victory. It means crying out, "O God, don't let me do this again!" David prayed this way: "Create in me a pure heart, O God, and renew a steadfast spirit within me" (Psalm 51:10). In asking for a new heart, we realize the need for sanctification, the power not to sin.

In our Christian walk, we will sin. But our desires, because of Christ, have changed. In fact, we have come to hate sin, especially in ourselves. Our desire is now for purity and holiness. If that desire is not in you, then you've never fully dealt with sin in your life. All too many Christians short-circuit the process of repentance and stop before they get to this point. If you are actively engaged in sin, please ask the Lord for strength to confess it, repent of it, and renounce it once and for all!

What happens in us after we have gone through this process of confession and repentance? David's response to forgiveness was to experience a restoration of joy and praise. "Restore to me the joy of your salvation and grant me a willing spirit, to sustain me" (Psalm 51:12 NIV). God's people are a forgiven people who have something to shout about, and who have a reason for joy. Peter writes, "But you are a chosen people, a royal priesthood, a holy nation, a people belonging to God, that you may declare the praises of him who called you out of darkness into his wonderful light" (1 Peter 2:9 NIV). Praise is what forgiven people do!

LEARN to Encounter Jesus

God made him who had no sin to be sin for us, so that in him we might become the righteousness of God. (2 Corinthians 5:21, NIV)

Reflect on the reason Christ became sin—or, more personally, for *whom* did He suffer and give His life on Calvary? Listen as Jesus whispers these words to your soul, "I did it for you. I did it for you!" The One who knew no sin became sin for you and for me (2 Corinthians 5:21). Allow yourself to respond to this glorious truth. Is your heart moved with wonder, humility, and joy? Do gratitude and praise fill your soul? Share these feelings with God.

Lord, I am so grateful that _____.

David even goes beyond worship in his response to the forgiveness of God. He did not keep what God had done bottled up inside him. He had been forgiven, and he wanted the world to know it. He declared, "Then I will teach transgressors your ways, and sinners will turn back to you" (Psalm 51:13 NIV). If we are going to be effective in sharing the gospel, it's going to be because we really believe that God has done something tremendous in our lives and we want that to happen in others' lives, too.

How do you deal with sin in your life? God has provided the answer to your sins in the person of Jesus. He doesn't want a single one of us to walk around burdened by sin. Perhaps right now is the time to bring your sins to the only One who can deal with them. Church attendance won't cleanse you from sin. Ministry and acts of service won't take care of your sin. Only Jesus can do that. God is calling the church to repentance! Turn from sin! Agree with God about the sinfulness of your sin. Ask for forgiveness. Trust in the cleansing blood of Jesus to provide not only forgiveness, but also the power to avoid sin in the future. Begin today to sing the praises of the One who has washed you and made you clean forever.

 ## SHARE with Others in Community

Look back over your journey with Jesus. How have you experienced His forgiveness? How did He cleanse you, and how have you experienced His great love?

Tell another person your story of gratitude for God's forgiveness. Celebrate the changes God has made in you and give Him praise. Your words might begin something like this: "I am incredibly grateful for God's forgiveness. I can't imagine what my life would have been without His mercy."

 ## LOVE Others in Community

Ask the Lord to give you an opportunity to tell your story of forgiveness to a person who doesn't yet have a relationship with Jesus. Listen to their story. Ask permission to tell your story with words such as these: "I still have a long way to go, but I am grateful for the changes God has made in my life so far. His forgiveness has made all the difference in the world. Do you mind if I share my story with you?"

6

ON OUR KNEES
From *Seizing the Future on Our Knees*
by Doug Beacham

CRY OUT TO THE LORD
*Lord, I don't ever want to underestimate my sin,
but I want to stand clean before You all the days of
my life. I want my sinful actions, behaviors, and
choices to be washed away by Your love and by Your
mercy. I praise You for being a God who lavishly
gives the gift of forgiveness to those who ask.*

PREFACE

Change will come to our lives and our communities when there
is a common resolve to corporately join together before the face
of God to be reconciled from sin and to seek God's will for our
future. This change will come when we experience both times of
confession and repentance, admission of sin and our decision to
live life differently. Let's look, with perhaps a fresh perspective, at
our need for God's abundant grace.

*If my people, who are called by my name, will humble themselves and pray
and seek my face and turn from their wicked ways, then I will hear from
heaven and will forgive their sin and will heal their land.*
(2 Chronicles 7:14, NIV)

THE SIN OF THE ELDER BROTHER SYNDROME

No story confronts us with the Father's love like the parable of the prodigal son and his older brother. In this illustration, Jesus contrasts God's boundless love with the total ineptness of human affection. Both the prodigal and his brother needed the embrace of a forgiving father and a sense of "coming home." The younger brother undoubtedly needed the grace of a father after he came to his senses. He had selfishly demanded from his father, squandered precious gifts and lived a life of self-indulgence and rebellion. The difficult point of the parable, however, is the older son, who believed that by "staying at home" he deserved priority treatment. His refusal to join the celebration revealed his flawed understanding of the father's love. It also exposed the brother's pride, because he considered himself more worthy than his prodigal sibling.

Knowing that God has called us (the church) to unity and that the Father sees no distinction of sin, we must acknowledge the sin of the elder brother. The church today often looks much like this older sibling. In fact, the "elder brother syndrome" has caused us to resist God's love rather than rejoice in seeing it lavished upon penitent prodigals. This syndrome opens the door to anger, bitterness, jealousy, and complaint. Old resentments, rooted in pride, intensify our withdrawal from God and His family and deepen divisions that dishonor and wound others.

The elder brother's self-reliance reveals a spiritual poverty which closes the door to communion with the Father and fellowship with His family. Like the elder brother, we have hardened our hearts against those who have left us and wanted to come home. We have often failed to demonstrate that God is full of grace and mercy. Instead, we have manifested a spirit of legalism that is based on works. We remember offenses and forget the love and generosity of the Father.

Consider your need for confession and repentance from the Elder Brother Syndrome.

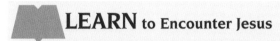

LEARN to Encounter Jesus

And while he was still a long way off, his father saw him coming. Filled with love and compassion, he ran to his son, embraced him, and kissed him. (Luke 15:20)

Even now, as you consider again the story of the prodigal son, the elder brother, and the father, allow the Lord to sensitize your heart to the true character of Father God. Spend some time meditating on this passage of Scripture. Ponder not only the story itself, but also the ways in which the heart of the Lord is revealed.

Meditate specifically on Luke 15:20 and imagine that Christ is waiting for you to return home, sometimes as the prodigal and sometimes as the elder brother. When He sees you in the distance, He is moved with compassion in spite of your selfishness, self-reliance, pride, condemnation, and sin; He *runs* toward you, even when you're a long way off.

If you have demonstrated the sin of the elder brother, rest assured that when the Father sees you, He smiles with complete joy. In spite of your arrogance, bitterness, and resentment, He leaps quickly off the front porch because He cannot wait to be with you. The Father embraces you, kisses you, and whispers in your ear. He does not offer lectures or criticism. There is no rebuke or scorn. His voice is filled with compassion as He embraces you and tells you that He loves you. There's a ring, a robe, and the announcement of a huge party. The true character of God is One who welcomes you with outstretched arms, is ready to embrace you, and is excited to love you.

Allow the Holy Spirit to fill your heart with gratitude for the grace that you have received. Ask Him to bring you to a time of fresh reflection upon the grace of the embracing Christ. Pray that He would fill you with wonder for His care and gratefulness for His love.

Forgive me, Father, for all the ways the elder brother syndrome has worked in my heart. Fill my heart, Holy Spirit, with the wonder of an embracing, welcoming Jesus; may my joy and gratitude for being so loved empower my humility and grace-filled giving to others.

The Sin of Judgmentalism

We have read our Lord's warning not to judge lest we be judged, yet have judged. We have judged unbelievers, hindering their entrance into the kingdom of God. We have judged faults in the lives of our brothers and sisters in Christ. We have often emphasized outward appearance, rather than the condition of the heart. Our judgmentalism has excluded people from the church.

Judgmentalism has broken our fellowship with other members of the body of Christ. It has caused us to confuse personal convictions with the eternal principles of God's Word. Judgmentalism has given birth to the sin of hypocrisy and put people into bondage to traditions instead of freeing them to minister. We have often overemphasized the negative, while neglecting positive ministries such as worship, witness, and service to others.

Consider your own need for confession and repentance from judgmentalism.

 PRAY and **Experience Scripture**

But if we confess our sins to him, he is faithful and just to forgive us our sins and to cleanse us from all wickedness. (1 John 1:9)

Prayerfully consider the sin of judgmentalism. Could there be any evidence of this sin in your own life? Talk to the heavenly Father, confessing and turning to Him, asking for His forgiveness.

Heavenly Father, it is wrong of me to_____. I know that part of the reason why You had to die was because of my_____. And I know that my sin hurts You. And I ask for Your forgiveness for this area of my life.

Jesus embraces you. He forgives you and declares His love for you. In spite of the sin you have just shared, the Savior sees you as a person worthy of His love, acceptance, and grace. And just like the woman in the gospel of John, Jesus says, "Where are your accusers?… Neither do I [accuse you]. Go and sin no more" (John 8:10–11).

How might Jesus want to free you from judging others? Talk to the Lord in prayer.

I want to thank You, Jesus, for not withholding love from me or judging me. I praise You for Your love that was expressed toward me and I pray that I might become more like You. Holy Spirit, deliver me from judging others and equip me to better express the love of Jesus to those around me.

THE SIN OF SPIRITUAL PRIDE

The original sin was pride. Lucifer exalted himself against God and brought sin into the universe (Ezekiel 28:11–19). The sin of pride was introduced into the human family when Adam and Eve yielded to Satan's temptation. Man still exalts himself and declares his independence from God. This temptation often seduces the Church.

Pride deceived us so that we have tried to accomplish God's work in our own strength instead of in the power of the Holy Spirit. We have sought our glory instead of giving all glory to Him. Pride has caused us to contend with one another rather than edify the church. It has caused the heavens to be as iron and earth as brass, rendering our labors unfruitful.

Consider your need for confession and repentance from pride.

 SHARE with Others in Community

You can pray for anything, and if you have faith, you will receive it you. (Matthew 21:22)

Talk with a friend, family member, or mentor about your own tendencies toward pride. Be vulnerable with your story. When you are done sharing your story, then pray together. Quietly listen before the Lord as His Spirit speaks to you about areas of your life that need to look more like our humble Savior. Ask the Lord to give you discernment and direction as you respond to the following:

Lord, I sense a needed fresh work of humility in me, particularly toward _____ *(which person or persons in your life?). Free me from pride. I want to only seek Your glory.*

✝ Lord, forgive me, as there have been times that I have had a superior attitude and taken Your grace for granted. I want Your Spirit to stir within me a humble and grateful heart. Overwhelm me with a deep awareness of my identity as the beloved of God and then constrain and control me through the grateful wonder of Your love.

 ## LOVE Others in Community

Ask God to show you a person in your community who could benefit from a grace-filled, accepting response. Look for opportunities to demonstrate these gifts to another person.

Heavenly Father, I want to demonstrate the same welcoming embrace to others that You have shown me. Help me see people in my world this week who could benefit from this kind of love.

7

GODLY SORROW: KEY TO REPENTANCE

From *Godly Sorrow Produces Repentance*
by David Ferguson

CRY OUT TO THE LORD

Lord, I cry out to You today. I ask that You would break my heart with what breaks Yours. I want to know the things about my life that bring sorrow to Your heart. Your Word says that godly sorrow produces repentance, so I pray that You would produce godly sorrow within me for my sinful ways. Let godly sorrow produce a deep and lasting repentance in me.

PREFACE

It's a certain promise, a bold declaration: Godly sorrow produces repentance. In a day when true life change seems elusive and any Christlike distinction seems lost in our culture, this is good news indeed. In the midst of continuing to do the very things we don't want to do, the promise regarding repentance is refreshing (Romans 7:15).

In 2 Corinthians we read about Paul's burden for the Corinthians. It is not the outcome of repentance that grips the apostle's heart, but rather the godly sorrow that produces, prompts, and brings forth this genuine repentance. He writes, "For the sorrow that is according to the will of God produces repentance without regret, leading to salvation, but the sorrow of the world produces death" (2 Corinthians 7:10–11, NASB).

Before there is evidence of a changed life, there must be an internal work of godly sorrow. A deep, emotional work of the heart must precede a change of behavior, attitude, and action. In his first letter, Paul challenged the Corinthians to a brokenness of heart. In the second letter to the Corinthians, the apostle rejoiced with the believers over the positive changes in their lives. Godly sorrow must have done its work in the lives of this early church!

In contrast to the sorrow of the world, godly sorrow is timeless and eternal. In this world, we experience tribulation and trials; struggles and losses take their toll. We constantly deal with the reality of rejection, regrets, disappointments, and pain. The good news is that we're not left alone in this journey. We have a Great High Priest who has gone before us (Hebrews 4:15), who was Himself acquainted with grief (Isaiah 53:3), and is even sitting at the right hand of God interceding for us now (Hebrews 7:25). Additionally, through the provision of divine comfort we can experience blessing in the midst of our sorrows when we receive comfort from God and other people (Matthew 5:4; 2 Corinthians 1:2–4). Still, this sorrow, as deep and penetrating as it is, can't compare to the power of godly sorrow.

So what's the difference between godly sorrow and the sorrow we experience in our world? First, godly sorrow is His sorrow. This kind of sorrow belongs to God, but it can be revealed, shared, and imparted to the attentive hearts of His children.

The Reason for Godly Sorrow

Godly sorrow speaks of His pain; God's heart actually feels sorrow. You may never have considered it before, but our God has experienced the emotion of sorrow. Remember the pain of our heavenly Father as He was rejected by His created hosts (Isaiah 14:12–14)? Recall how our God was betrayed in the garden by the "very good" of His creation (Genesis 3). Remember how God was repeatedly forsaken and abandoned by His people (Exodus 32:7–10)? Surely there was a sorrow-filled heart behind these words: "Then the Lord saw that the wickedness of man was great on the earth, and that every intent of the thoughts of his heart was only evil continually. The Lord was sorry that He had made man on the earth, and He was grieved in His heart" (Genesis 6:5–6 NASB).

To experience godly sorrow means to share in the Father's pain—the pain of a loving Father who for us would:

- Watch Him who knew no sin become sin (2 Corinthians 5:21).
- Allow the perfect One to be wounded, bruised, and chastised (Isaiah 53:4–5).
- Hear His only Son utter these words: "My God, My God, why have you abandoned me?" (Matthew 27:46).

As we consider God's experiences of sorrow, it ought to soften our heart with compassion and bring us to quiet brokenness. After all, *why* did God allow all of the experiences described above? Gratefully, it was for a relationship with you and me. God watched His son beaten and crucified and chose this great sorrow for our salvation. But then we must ask the question: *Why* did God have to send His Son to die and experience this great sorrow? It was for our sin that Christ had to die. And therefore it was our sin that contributed to God's sorrow. Our sin hurt Jesus and it is our sin that has broken the heart of God. What a contrast? The world's sorrow focuses on *our* grief and what *we've* experienced. Godly sorrow shatters this self-focus, and challenges a heart to ponder: *What have I done to the Father and His Son?*

 **LEARN** to Encounter Jesus

I want to know Christ and experience the mighty power that raised him from the dead. I want to suffer with him, sharing in his death. (Philippians 3:10)

Quietly meditate on the words "suffer with Him." Bring your mind and heart to focus upon Him. Ask the Holy Spirit to center your heart on Him. It was Jesus who became *your* sin. He was bruised for *you*; He was beaten for *you*. Ask the Holy Spirit to soften your heart and to move you with compassion for His sufferings.

Lord Jesus, You took my penalty; You suffered for me. I have a fresh perspective of how my sin hurt You. Heavenly Father, I see also that my sin hurt You. Because I needed redemption, Your heart was filled with sorrow. My heart is now moved with _____ . *I am heartbroken that I was a part of God's sorrow and Christ's suffering. Bring this image to my mind often. I want to share in this suffering.*

THE RECEIVING OF GODLY SORROW

The Father is ready to vulnerably reveal His heart and His pain, but He only trusts His sorrow-filled heart to those who can be still enough to know Him. Those who are busy or pre-occupied will miss Him. Those who are cavalier or think light of their sin won't hear Him. Sorrow is not a rational concept that's to be dissected, discussed, and debated as doctrine. It's a personal experience between a Father and a loved one, a tender issue of the heart, an emotional issue of the soul.

Godly sorrow comes by way of the Spirit's conviction and my confession. Only the Spirit can convict (John 16:8), and only I can confess (1 John 1:9; James 5:16). The Holy Spirit will fulfill His role of convicting me of selfishness, pride, disrespect, or other specific offenses toward God and others. And then comes our part: genuine confession. We must say the same thing about our selfishness, pride, or disrespect that the Father says. We must say more than a mere intellectual agreement of wrong doing or a volitional voicing of regret. Confession is our *emotional expression* of godly sorrow. With a humble spirit and a contrite heart, we voice our agreement with the Father's sorrow:

- God, it was Your Son who was wounded for my transgressions, my selfishness and pride.
- It was Your Son who was bruised for my iniquities, my criticalness and disrespect.
- God, against You and You only have I sinned.
- It was because of my sin that You had to hear those soul-piercing words, "My God, My God, why have You abandoned Me?"

Confession from this kind of heart ushers in godly sorrow. No longer is there self-defense, pretense, or posturing—only a broken and contrite heart.

PRAY and Experience Scripture

For the sorrow that is according to the will of God produces repentance….(2 Corinthians 7:10, NASB)

It's the Father's sorrowed heart and He can share it with you. Ask the Holy Spirit to reveal how your sin has contributed to the Father's sorrow.

Holy Spirit, touch me with a broken and contrite heart, especially as I consider my sin of _____. *In a fresh way, show me how this has saddened Your heart. Remind me often of how my sin hurt Jesus and my sin hurts You. Change me, because I love You and don't want to hurt You in this way any longer.*

THE RESULTS OF GODLY SORROW

The results of this kind of frequent encounter with God bring both internal and external changes. We no longer have to grit our teeth and try to be different. Change comes gently and supernaturally because the love of Christ starts to control or constrain our lives (2 Corinthians 5:14). It's these loving encounters with a God who's experienced sorrow that produces the power to change us. A grateful rejoicing occurs when we experience true, godly sorrow because our confession frees us of guilt. Godly sorrow also produces a joy in being forgiven and grateful thanksgiving ushers me into worship.

Godly sorrow produces repentance—changes that make me more and more like Christ. An experience with God's sorrow makes a lasting impression on our lives because we have been *with* Him. Having entered into the fellowship of His sufferings, having shared intimately with Him in His sorrow, we can never be the same again!

 # SHARE with Others in Community

Now that you have reflected on your experience of godly sorrow, can you serve the Lord with the gladness of your heart (Psalm 100:2)? Pause quietly in worship, and take time to tell God about the gladness of your heart and your gratitude for how He has forgiven you of your sins. Make plans to share this with a friend, mentor, or a small group.

God, I am grateful for Your grace and undeserved favor. Thank You that Your sorrow has broken my heart and will bring about change deep within me. I can't wait to look more like Jesus, so I can live a life that pleases You and brings glory to Your name.

Plan to talk about this experience with a friend, mentor, or small group. Your words might begin like this: *I've come to know God in a fresh way. I've experienced the sorrow of God's heart and how He hurt because of my* _____.

 # LOVE Others in Community

Ask God to give you an opportunity to talk about the changes He is making in your life. Look for times to talk about the power of godly sorrow and how it brings about repentance. Your words might sound something like this: *I have so many things that need to change about my life, but I'm hopeful because God really is changing me. I recently discovered how my wrong choices hurt God. This experience changed something in me.* Then go on to share about your experience.

8

REVIVAL REALITY

From *One Cry: A Nationwide Call for Spiritual Awakening*
by Byron Paulus and Bill Elliff

CRY OUT TO THE LORD

*Lord, I cry out to You. Take a look at my life,
and help me to see and put away the things
in my life that don't look like You and that are
not pleasing in Your sight. I'm asking You to grow
me up, and to bring maturity and more and more
Christlikeness into my life for Jesus' sake.*

PREFACE

Repentance is a deep Spirit-wrought change of mind that produces a change of direction in a person's life. It is coming to realize what you've lost and what you so desperately need. It is seeing the value once again of simple and pure devotion to Jesus Christ. Not only that, but repentance is taking your eyes off valueless gods and peering again into the face of Christ. It's nothing short of falling in love all over again. And when we begin to do that, then God draws near and begins to show Himself powerful in our lives and in the lives of others.

Remember

"Remember from where you have fallen, and repent…" (Revelation 2:5, NASB).

If we need to repent, it is because we have turned. Once, our gaze was fixed on the face of Christ. We looked to Him, loved Him, and would do anything for Him. But somewhere along the way, something else captured our attention. It could be the material things of this world, or the love of comfort and pleasure, or the pursuit of prestige and reputation—the lust to have everyone like us. When our eyes shift, our direction changes. Often, before we even realize what has happened, the world has captured our attention and we have turned our backs toward Christ.

That is why *remembering*, looking back, is so important. When we remember from where we've fallen and the marvelous joy of intimacy with Christ, we are willing to repent. Real repentance is not driven as much by what we turn *from* as what we turn *to*. We long to come back home, and then we begin to turn in that direction by the grace of God.

Sometimes repentance happens in a moment. But for most of us, going home is a process. It can be sped along by spending concentrated, intentional time with Him. We may need to take deliberate time to listen to what He is saying through His precious Word. Maybe we need to sit with an open notebook and ask God to show us every false god that has garnered our attention and every sin that has flowed from that idol worship. Perhaps we need to fast to quiet the noise of other gods and humble our soul through this invaluable, forgotten exercise. Whatever it takes, we must pay the price to make the turn home to His heart.

Why not take the time now to voice your repentance? Wouldn't you like to slip your hand in His again…and come back home?

PRAY and Experience Scripture

Therefore, since we have so great a cloud of witnesses surrounding us, let us also lay aside every encumbrance and the sin which so easily entangles us….(Hebrews 12:1, NASB)

Pause quietly in an attitude of humble repentance before the Lord. Ask Him to show you the places in your life that are childish, immature, or weighing down your pursuit of Christlikeness.

Lord, show me the places in my life that are keeping me from being more like You. Show me the childish parts of my life that hinder me from Christlikeness. Reveal the sins that reflect my immaturity and lack of growth. Lord, I'm ready to hear You, repent of my wrongdoings, and walk in newness of life.

Be still and wait for the Lord to speak to you. Listen as the Holy Spirit reveals what He desires. We know that "he hears us whenever we ask for anything that pleases him. And since we know he hears us when we make our requests, we also know that he will give us what we ask for" (1 John 5:14–15). Therefore, take the next few moments to confess to the Lord and ask Him to change you.

Lord, I admit that there are parts of my life that are childish, immature, and sinful. I know that my _____ is keeping me from becoming more like You. I know it must hurt Your heart to see this in my life, because You love me and want what's best for me. Please forgive me and cleanse me. Change me. Make me different. Help me put this out of my life so I can be pleasing in Your sight.

RETURN

"Remember from where you have fallen, and repent and do the deeds you did at first…" (Revelation 2:5, NASB).

When we are cooperating with God in His gracious work of personal revival, we return to Him. And with that return, good works begin to flow from our relationship. What kind of deeds? The joyful actions of crazy, reckless, extravagant love!

Remember the first time you fell in love with someone? The long phone calls? The homemade cards? The gift you bought that you couldn't afford? There is no prescription for this same kind of extravagant love in our spiritual walk because different people express their love in different ways. There are some indicators however, that are universal when we fall head over heels in love with Christ. The following are some of the signs of a revived heart.

TIME

When you love Christ you don't ignore Him. You want to spend time with Him daily. When He wakes you up earlier than expected in the morning, or keeps you up all night, you remember that He wants to speak to you, love you, and equip you. And because you remember, you joyfully give Him the precious gift of time.

TALK

Revived people commune with the One they love. They talk and listen intently with Him through the Word and prayer. You learn what it means to "pray without ceasing" (1 Thessalonians 5:17) because you can't stand to be away from Him and you see the value of His leadership and input on every decision. There are even moments when you just love to sit in His presence and tell

Him you love Him. You love to talk with Him privately and in a group with others. A revived believer prays.

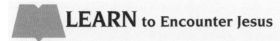

LEARN to Encounter Jesus

Listen and talk to Jesus right now. Reflect again on the parts of your life that keep you from looking like Jesus. Are you weary of their impact on your life? Tell the Lord about these things and then listen to His invitation: "Come to me, all you who are weary and burdened, and I will give you rest" (Matthew 11:28).

Jesus invites us to come to Him in our weariness. Maybe you are weary of sinful ways; perhaps you are weary of seeking fulfillment in what you have acquired, achieved, or accomplished; maybe you are weary of succumbing to the world's demands; or perhaps you are weary of trying to live in your own strength, wisdom, or power—if any of those describe you, then come to the Lord today and pray.

Lord Jesus, I am tired of _____. My heart is weary because of _____. As I meditate on the wonder of Your forgiveness, and Your promise of rest, my heart is filled with _____. I want to return to more times of intimacy with You because I know that's where I will find strength and renewal for my soul.

TESTIMONY

People who are in love are almost obnoxious as they talk about their beloved. The greatest reason most believers don't share Christ with others is that they have nothing to say. It has been a long time since they had a life-changing encounter with Christ.

There is no desire (only a dull sense of duty) to witness to others or give testimony of God's goodness or deliverance. But when you are revived, you cannot help but speak about what you've seen and heard (Acts 4:20). You are unashamed of Him. In humility, you don't think less of yourself—you just think of yourself less and you talk of Him more. When your heart is *filled* with Him, your mouth will *speak* of Him.

TREASURES

When you see Christ afresh, you remember that every single thing you have—indeed, every breath—is a gift from a gracious Father. You find yourself surrendering everything back into His control. When He tells you to fill up someone's car with gas, or pay for someone's meal, you do it gladly. You are moved by the needs of others because Christ's compassion is constraining you and you long for them to know His blessing and salvation. Selfishness is superseded by love-driven generosity. You become like the One you're gazing at, for He is the ultimate giver.

 SHARE with Others in Community

Pause to consider that God's ultimate purpose for your life is intimacy with Him as He transforms you into the likeness of Christ, which allows you to receive of God's abundant love and gives you access to intimate fellowship, which also enables you to bless others with His love and empowers your witness of Jesus.

What do these truths do to your heart? Pray with a prayer partner. Express your thanksgiving together as a way to love and honor the Lord. "He who offers a sacrifice of thanksgiving honors Me" (Psalm 50:23, NASB). Your prayers might begin like this:

Lord, as I consider how You love me and how You want to change me so that we can experience even closer fellowship, I feel thankful because _____. *Lord, as I consider how You love me and want to give me the power to love others well, I am thankful because* _____.

➡ LOVE others in Community

Finally, ask the Lord to show you a person who could benefit from your vulnerability. As an expression of your love, who might need to hear your confession about the area of growth that Jesus has revealed? Ask the Holy Spirit to reveal this person to you and then plan your confession.

Holy Spirit, I know You have spoken to me about putting away certain things in my life. I sense that You want me to put away _____. *Who has been negatively impacted by this sin in my life and could benefit from my confession?*

Plan to share your confession to the person whom the Holy Spirit reveals. Your confession might sound like: "I am committed to putting things out of my life that aren't pleasing to God. He's recently shown me an area where I need to change and that's my_____. I'm wondering if you have been negatively impacted by this. If so, I want to know about it and make it right. I've asked God's forgiveness for this and I would like to ask you to forgive me as well."

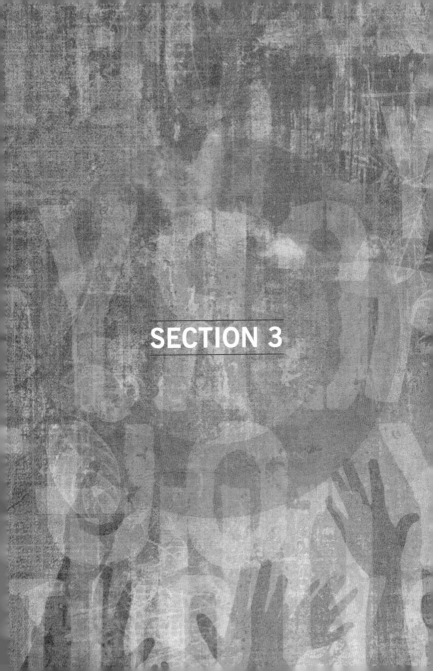

SECTION 3

I YIELD TO HIS LORDSHIP AND THE SPIRIT'S FULLNESS

Hear my cry, O God,
listen to my prayer;
from the end of the earth I call to you
when my heart is faint.
Lead me to the rock
that is higher than I.
(Psalm 61:1–2 ESV)

A SPIRIT-EMPOWERED FAITH

yields to the Holy Spirit's fullness as life in the Spirit brings supernatural intimacy with the Lord, manifestation of divine gifts, and witness of the fruit of the Spirit. Let these authors encourage your Spirit-empowered faith:

- Mark Batterson—Throw Down Your Staff
- Frances Chan—Life in the Spirit
- Kay Horner—A Call to Sacrifice
- Tom Phillips—Revival Signs

9

THROW DOWN YOUR STAFF

From *Wild Goose Chase*
by Mark Batterson

CRY OUT TO THE LORD

Lord, I cry out to You today for Your grace and mercy. I need Your help to throw down any label, belief, or image of myself that doesn't come from You. I know that to live a life that is empowered by Your Spirit, I must let go of anything You ask of me. Give me the grace to let go of what You're asking me to, and give me the strength to live a life that pleases You.

PREFACE

Living a life of Spirit-empowered adventure will require leaving behind the routine, the humdrum, and the status quo. A life of empowerment may mean turning loose the things that make sense or fall in line with human standards. A life with the Spirit means we're on a divine exploration, following the path that God has laid down for us, even though we oftentimes don't know where we are going when we begin. Sometimes following that path requires great risks, while at other times it means we respond to the simplest promptings in our heart. Either way, we know that we are living for God's glory because we are choosing to follow His promptings.

Every summer I take a six-week preaching sabbatical. The reason is simple. It is so easy to get focused on what God wants to do through me that I totally neglect what God wants to do in me. So I take off my sandals for six weeks. I go on vacation. I go to church with my family. And for several weeks during the summer, I just sit with our congregation, taking notes and singing songs like everyone else. My sabbatical is one way I keep the routine from becoming routine. But it's about more than just taking off my sandals. Let me explain.

Shortly after telling Moses to take off his sandals, God gave Moses one more curious command. He told Moses to throw down his staff.

> Then the LORD said to him, "What is that in your hand?" "A staff," he replied. The LORD said, "Throw it on the ground." Moses threw it on the ground and it became a snake, and he ran from it. Then the LORD said to him, "Reach out your hand and take it by the tail." So Moses reached out and took hold of the snake and it turned back into a staff in his hand. "This," said the LORD, "is so that they may believe that the LORD, the God of their fathers—the God of Abraham, the God of Isaac and the God of Jacob—has appeared to you." (Ex. 4:2–5)

A shepherd's staff was a six-foot-long wooden rod that was curved at one end. It functioned as a walking stick, a weapon, and a prod used to guide the flock. Moses never left home without his staff. That staff symbolized his security. It offered him physical security from wild animals. It provided his financial security—his sheep were his financial portfolio. And it was a form of relational security. After all, Moses worked for his father-in-law.

But the staff was more than just a form of security. It was also part of his identity. When Moses looked in the mirror, he saw a shepherd—nothing more, nothing less. And I think that's why Moses asked God to send someone else. "Who am I, that I should go to Pharaoh and bring the Israelites out of Egypt?" (Ex. 3:11). I love the way God answers his question by changing the focus. God says: "I will be with you." (Ex. 3:12). That doesn't really seem like an answer to Moses' question, does it? But I think it was God's way of saying who you are isn't the issue; the issue is whose you are!

LEARN to Encounter Jesus

This is real love—not that we loved God, but that he loved us and sent his Son as a sacrifice to take away our sins. (1 John 4:10)

There is no greater love than to lay down one's life for one's friends. (John 15:13)

Jesus' sacrifice on the cross serves as a declaration of our immense worth in God's eyes. Imagine that Christ is speaking to you from heaven. Listen to the words that are just for you: *You are especially valuable to Me. You represent My thoughts, My personality, and what's important to Me. You are important to Me—so important that I laid down My life for you. I saw that you were in danger of being separated from Me for all of eternity, so I acted. I rescued you because I love you and couldn't bear the thought of a relationship without you. That's how I see you: one who is worth My sacrifice.*

Now respond to this declaration.

> Lord, when I hear Your declaration of my worth to you, I feel
> _____. Thank You for reminding me of the truth that
> my worth can only be declared by the One who created me and died
> for me.

Has God ever called you to throw something down? Something in which you find your security or put your identity? It's awfully hard to let go, isn't it? It feels like you are jeopardizing your future. And it feels like you could lose what is most important to you. But that is when you discover who you really are.

I agonize with you because I know how tough it is to throw down a staff. It was so hard to throw down my scholarship at the University of Chicago. It was so hard to leave the security of friends and family and move from Chicago to Washington DC. But the only way you discover a new identity is by letting an old one go. And the only way you'll find your security in Christ is by throwing down the human securities we tend to cling to.

PRAY and Experience Scripture

In reference to your former manner of life, you lay aside the old self....(Ephesians 4:22)

Ask the Holy Spirit to reveal the "staff" that you need to "throw down."

Lord, do I need to throw down

- a source of security or provision that's other than You?
- a label that I give myself or identity that's other than what You have declared?
- a habit or behavior that's contrary to Your plan for my life?

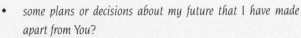

There is a branch of history called counterfactual theory that asks the what-if questions. So here's my counterfactual question: What if Moses had held on to his staff? I think the answer is simple: The shepherd's staff would have remained a shepherd's staff. I don't think God would have used Moses to deliver Israel. I think Moses would have gone right back to shepherding his flock.

If you aren't willing to throw down your staff, you forfeit the miracle that is at your fingertips. You have to be willing to let go of an old identity in order to take on a new identity. And that is what happens to Moses. This is a miracle of transformation. Not just the staff turning into a snake, but a shepherd of sheep turning into the leader of a nation. But Moses had to throw down the shepherd's staff in order for it to be transformed into the rod of God.

As far as we know, this is the first miracle Moses ever experienced. If Moses had held on to the staff, he would have forfeited all of those miracles. He would have spent the rest of his life counting sheep.

Where do you find your identity? What is the source of your security? Is it a title? A paycheck? A relationship? A degree? A name? There is nothing wrong with any of those things as long as you can throw them down.

If you find your security outside of Christ, you have a false sense of security. And you have a false sense of identity. As long as you hold on to your staff, you'll never know what you could have accomplished with God's help. And let me remind you of this: Your success isn't contingent upon what's in your hand. Your success is contingent upon whether God extends His mighty hand on your behalf.

So let me issue a challenge. Throw down your staff, and discover the adventure on the far side of routine.

 # SHARE with Others in Community

Restart your adventure with the Lord. Pray to Him now.

God, I am humbled by Your declaration of my identity and how I am worth the gift of Your Son. I am committed to laying aside anything that's not from You, specifically _____.

Share this insight with a friend, family member, or mentor. *I plan to tell* _____ *about God's declaration of our worth and how I am asking Him to help me throw down my "staff" daily.*

 # LOVE Others in Community

Ask the Holy Spirit to show you a person who is outside of a relationship with Jesus, but who could benefit from God's declaration of their identity. Ask God to reveal and make plans to affirm this truth in his or her life.

God, show me a person in my life who needs to hear about Your declaration of their worth. Help me know how to affirm that truth in them.

10

LIFE IN THE SPIRIT

From *Forgotten God*
by Francis Chan

CRY OUT TO THE LORD

Lord, I don't want to settle for the closeness I have with You now. I know there's more—a lot more. I want more of Your Spirit's closeness, more intimacy with You, more Christlike transformation, and more power in my life. I'm crying out for more of You, Jesus, for I know there is so much more to be had.

PREFACE

May our desire to experience more of the Holy Spirit be our starting point, not our endgame. And may we open our hearts and lives to His presence and action more fully than we have ever done before. By the power and presence of the Holy Spirit, we can be a people who live a life of transformation and power—a life that clearly points to the One who deserves all of our praise. It is by the power of the Holy Spirit that we are progressively made into the image and likeness of Christ, and it is by His might that we are empowered to live the life Jesus called us to live.

You might think that calling the Holy Spirit the "forgotten God" is a bit extreme. Maybe you agree that the church has focused too much attention elsewhere, but feel it is an exaggeration to say we have *forgotten* about the Spirit. I don't think so.

From my perspective, the Holy Spirit is tragically neglected and, for all practical purposes, forgotten. While no evangelical would deny His existence, I'm willing to bet there are millions of churchgoers across America who cannot confidently say they have experienced His presence or action in their lives over the past year. And many of them do not believe they can.

There is a big gap between what we read in Scripture about the Holy Spirit and how most believers and churches operate today. In many modern churches, you would be stunned by the apparent absence of the Spirit in any manifest way. And this, I believe, is the crux of the problem.

If I were Satan and my ultimate goal was to thwart God's kingdom and purposes, one of my main strategies would be to get churchgoers to ignore the Holy Spirit. The degree to which this has happened (and I would argue that it is a prolific disease in the body of Christ) is directly connected to the dissatisfaction most of us feel with and in the church. We understand something very important is missing. The feeling is so strong that some have run away from the church and God's Word completely.

→ LOVE Others in Community

Where the Spirit of the Lord is there is liberty. (2 Corinthians 3:17)

Tell someone your story about the times when you *have* experienced the presence of the Holy Spirit in your life. The times where *you have* experienced freedom and change, mean that these are the times you have surrendered and the Spirit of the Lord was present to work within you. Talk also about the additional areas of freedom and change that are still needed.

Holy Spirit, I want more and more of Your freedom in my life, especially in the area of _____. Show me what I need to surrender to You. I want to see and sense the Spirit of the Lord in my life in a real and powerful way.

I believe that this missing *something* in our church experience is actually a missing *Someone*—namely, the Holy Spirit. Without Him, people operate in their own strength and only accomplish human-size results. The world is not moved by love or actions that are of human creation. And the church is not empowered to live differently from any other gathering of people without the Holy Spirit. But when believers live in the power of the Spirit, the evidence in their lives is supernatural. The church cannot help but be different, and the world cannot help but notice.

My prayer is that your changed life would produce this kind of astonishment: "Now when they saw the boldness of Peter and John, and perceived that they were uneducated, common men, they were astonished. And they recognized that they had been with Jesus" (Acts 4:13).

PRAY and Experience Scripture

Let God transform you into a new person. (Romans 12:2)

Pause for a moment and ask the Holy Spirit to show you an area of your life that needs His transformation—specifically, a change that is needed that will only be explained by the work and presence of the Spirit of God. Ask God's Spirit to make such a change in you that others can't help but recognize that you have been with Jesus.

Holy Spirit, what part of my life needs to change today? What part of my life needs to change in such a way that people around me can't help but notice? Show me, Lord. And then empower that change within me. I want to be a beacon of transformation that points others to You.

No matter what religious tradition you come from, you likely carry baggage and harbor stereotypes when it comes to the Holy Spirit. It is going to require laying aside your baggage and stereotypes so you can be open to what God wants to teach you. Are you willing to do that?

Some people talk a lot about—even boast of—the Spirit, but their lives do not bear His fruit. Others speak of the Holy Spirit in theoretical or scholarly terms, yet do not experience Him at work. Still others ignore Him for all practical purposes and, as you might expect, rarely experience relationship or intimacy with the Spirit. And then there is that rare person who doesn't talk frequently about the Spirit, yet whose life is a powerful display of His presence and activity.

Some of you would like it if I said we were going to find a healthy balance between unhealthy extremes. That's not what we're going to do. Seeking a "healthy balance" of the Holy Spirit assumes that there are some who have too much Holy Spirit and others who have too little. I have yet to meet anyone with too much Holy Spirit. Granted, I've met many who talk about Him too much, but none who are actually overfilled with His presence.

As believers, we can never be "done" with God. He is infinite and we are finite; there will always be more of His character to discover, more of His love to experience, and more of His power to use for His purposes.

 ## SHARE with Others in Community

Ask the Spirit to remind you of a time when He was longing for you to reveal the fullness of His presence by loving others well. Then ask the Spirit to bring to mind some of the times when He wanted to you to share the work of the Spirit in your life, but you missed the opportunity.

Lord, speak to me about a time when You were longing for me to share Your love with others. I could have listened more to _____, *but I missed the opportunity. I could have apologized to* _____ *but I didn't. I could have helped more, but instead I* _____. *And I could have shared more appreciation, but instead I* _____.

As the Holy Spirit speaks to you, offer a humble prayer.

Lord, I want others to see the evidence of the work of Your Spirit in my life. I regret the times when I have missed Your prompting. Make me more sensitive to Your voice and empower my actions.

And perhaps the core issue is really about our holding back from giving ourselves to God, rather than our getting "too much" of Him. Perhaps when a person says I'd just like a little God, thank you very much," she or he is really saying I'd rather not give the parts of my life that I really care about over to God, so I'll just hold on to this, that, oh, and that, too.

It doesn't work that way. When I read Scripture, I see the truth and necessity of a life wholly surrendered to and dependent upon the Holy Spirit.

Paul wrote to the Corinthians that his words were not "wise and persuasive" but rather a "demonstration of the Spirit's power" in order that their faith "might not rest on men's wisdom, but on God's power" (1 Cor. 2:4–5 NIV). Later in the same letter he reiterates that "the kingdom of God is not a matter of talk but of power" (4:20 NIV).

I am tired of merely talking about God. I want to see God move through me, and through the worldwide body of Christ. I know there's more. We all know there's more. God has called us to more, through the presence and strength of the Holy Spirit. There's more of the Spirit and more of God than any of us is experiencing. I want to go there—not just intellectually, but in life, with everything that I am.

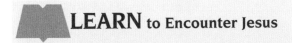

LEARN to Encounter Jesus

But I will send you the Advocate—the Spirit of truth. He will come to you from the Father and will testify all about me. (John 15:26).

Ask the Holy Spirit to be your Advocate. Ask Him to reveal *more of Jesus* as you reflect on the needs of your life and the circumstances of your world. What needs and challenges are you facing today where He can empower you to meet those needs and face those challenges?

Now ask the Holy Spirit to testify about the character of Jesus. Does the Spirit want you to know that Jesus is the all-powerful One, the Mighty Counselor, the Great I Am, the Prince of Peace, the Great Provider, the Attentive One, the Gracious One, or the Great Physician? One of the Spirit's jobs is to reveal more of Jesus.

Holy Spirit, given the needs of my life and the challenges of my world, what do You want to testify about Jesus? What do You want me to know about Him?

Listen as the Spirit testifies more about Him.

11

A CALL TO SACRIFICE
by Kay Horner

> ## CRY OUT TO THE LORD
> *Lord, I cry out to You because I want to know You more deeply. I want to experience more of Your love and its governance or control in my life.*
> (2 Corinthians 5:14)
> *I want to live a life that sacrifices my desires for Yours. Help me to be a person who sacrifices in order to fulfill Your will in my life.*

PREFACE

Ironically, one of the most critical ingredients for a vibrant faith in Jesus is a life of sacrifice. It's one of great paradoxes of our faith. To live a life of abundance requires our sacrifice—sacrifice of our agendas, our desires, and our ambitions for His. But when we learn to set aside our own will for the will and plans of God, that is when we truly live. True life cannot be experienced in Christ without sacrifice. When Jesus calls us to come to and follow Him, He calls us to lay down our lives in order for Christ to live through us.

Almost two thousand years have passed since the death and resurrection of our Lord. Yet, we still witness the powerful impact Christ's passion has in our world. Movies like *Son of God*, and *The Passion of the Christ*, give us a vivid reminder of the incredible suffering and shame our Savior endured to atone for our sins and reconcile us to the Father. We may question why these portrayals have to be so bloody and graphic; however, the scenes are clearly in the Gospels. Nearly one-third of each is devoted to the last week of Jesus' life. Blood and suffering are infused in the very foundations of the Christian faith.

We must embrace the shock and shame of the agonizing death of our Savior. We must sense the horror and heartache of the bloody payment for sin. Yet, we also experience unspeakable joy of the provision made possible through the wondrous cross. We embrace the crucifixion *and* the resurrection, the passion *and* the power, at the same time.

LEARN to Encounter Jesus

For God made Christ, who never sinned, to be the offering for our sin, so that we could be made right with God through Christ. (2 Corinthians 5:21)

Imagine Christ at Calvary. Recall the crucifixion scene. Meditate quietly on the day when Jesus became sin for us. Imagine hearing His words: "My God, My God, why have You forsaken Me?" Now remember *why* Jesus had to become sin—or more personally, who did He do this for? Why did Jesus go through all of the suffering on that dreadful day? Or more to the point, for *whom* did Jesus go through all of the pain and agony of Calvary? Why did Jesus have to feel the relational pain and abandonment of His heavenly Father? It was because of His love for *you*. In quiet reflection, say these words to yourself, He *did it for me.* He *did it for me.* Now take some time and respond to the Lord.

Jesus, when I remember how You went to Calvary because You loved me, my heart is filled with feelings of _____. Thank You, Lord, that You became sin so that I could be made right with God. My heart is overwhelmed at the way You sacrificed Yourself for me. Help me to live a life of sacrifice in response to You.

Years ago, I was privileged to see a pre-release viewing of *The Passion of the Christ* with a group of local pastors. I can't really describe what I felt and experienced both during and following this powerful depiction and unforgettable testament of my Lord's suffering. I became physically ill from the stress and emotion. While driving home from the theater, I reached into my handbag for something to relieve my headache. The Lord clearly spoke to my spirit, I *wasn't able to reach for an Excedrin Migraine. I suffered it all without any painkillers.*

If suffering and sacrifice are an integral part of Scripture and the life of Christ, the question we must ask ourselves is: "Are suffering and sacrifice a part of my life?" Spurgeon once wrote that he was "certain that he had never grown in grace one-half so much anywhere as upon the bed of pain."

Paul told the Romans: "We are heirs—heirs of God and co-heirs with Christ, if indeed we share in His sufferings in order that we may also share in His glory" (8:17 NIV). Somehow, our Western culture and consumer capitalism have convinced us that

God's grace is merely to make life a joy ride to heaven and that persecution and suffering either ended with the New Testament or they are limited to other countries.

German theologian Dietrich Bonhoeffer was well acquainted with suffering. He so eloquently wrote: "When Christ calls a man, He bids him come and die." In his book *The Cost of Discipleship*, Bonhoeffer reminds us, "Suffering, then, is the badge of true discipleship. The disciple is not above his master. Following Christ means, *passio passiva*, suffering because we have to suffer." A true follower of Christ is called to take up His cross. It is a call to allegiance to the suffering Christ; therefore, it is not at all surprising that Christians should be called upon to sacrifice.

 PRAY and Experience Scripture

I want to know Christ and the power of His resurrection and the fellowship of sharing in His sufferings….(Philippians 3:10, NASB)

Imagine the scene in the upper room when Jesus was more vulnerable with His disciples than ever before. Jesus foreshadows His death when He says, "This is My body that is broken for you." The Savior is tender and vulnerable, yet in the midst of this warmhearted moment the disciples fight over who is the greatest (Luke 22:24).

Take a moment to reflect on what the disciples' response did to the Savior's heart. Imagine how He must have felt at that moment. Begin to know Him and how He must have suffered, even in the upper room. How might you complete the following statement? "I imagine that Christ may have felt

_____."

What does it do to your heart that Jesus, the One who was wounded for our transgressions, experienced such insensitivity and rejection? Truly begin to fellowship with Him in His suffering. What does it do to your heart as you reflect on all that Jesus must have felt in the upper room? What do you feel for Jesus? "As I consider Christ's sorrow, my heart is touched with _____."

Now imagine that with a sorrowed heart, Jesus says the same things to you as He did with His disciples: "I see how people who don't know Me treat others. I don't want you to be like that." Pause to consider the heart of Christ as you hear Him utter these words: "Let it not be so among you." Is it possible that this is still the Savior's request? Could He still long to see a sacrificial difference in His disciples?

Respond to Jesus in prayer.

Jesus, I want to truly know You. I am sad and hurt that You experienced the painful things You did in the upper room and at Calvary. Make me different from the people of this world. I want my love for You to "constrain" me and prompt me to live differently.

The call resounding for Christ's church, especially in America, is the call to personal sacrifice. Not merely sacrifice for the sake of sacrifice or to claim I know Him in the fellowship of His suffering. The call is for the same reason that Christ suffered—that others might experience His resurrection life. Paul proclaimed: "I rejoice in my sufferings for you, and I am completing in my flesh what is lacking in Christ's afflictions for His body, that is, the church" (Colossians 1:24, HCSB).

We are not called to be God's pitiful people, too weak to break the chains of indifference that bind us to the status quo. We are called to be God's chosen people, empowered by God's grace and moving toward the promise of sacrificial love. The meaning of the cross and the meaning of life are witnessed through His willingness to sacrifice for others, to be hurt for others, to die for others. In Jesus' darkest hour, the voice of God breaks through, asking us the question: *Now do you understand how much I love you?*

 # SHARE with Others in Community

Share your renewed connection with the sufferings of Jesus with a friend, family member, or mentor. Celebrate the truth that we can actually fellowship with Jesus in these ways. Your words might sound like the following: "I have come to understand a little more about what it means to fellowship in His sufferings. I experienced more of what it means to hurt with Jesus when _____." Or, "This experience was so important to me because _____."

 # LOVE Others in Community

Ask the Lord how He might want you to be different from the people of the world. Does God want you to be more patient, kind, joyful, peaceful, faithful, gentle, loving, or self-controlled? Ask Jesus to reveal His desire specifically for you.

Lord, because of Your sacrifice for me, I want my life to look different from the people who don't know You as their Savior. How do You want my life to be different? Who needs to see this demonstration of the fruit of the Spirit in my life?

12

REVIVAL SIGNS

From *Revival Signs*
by Tom Phillips

CRY OUT TO THE LORD

*Lord, I cry out to You today for a powerful revival.
Sensitize my heart so that I am free to share
my life with others. Then empower me to share
Your good news with them too. Without Your
presence, there is no hope for a spiritual awakening.
I ask that You would rend the heavens and come
down; that Your presence would flood our
hearts and our lives in powerful ways.*

PREFACE

Look at any spiritual awakening in history, including those that
have occurred in our own country, and you'll discover an obvious,
common thread: Revival is always preceded by spiritual deadness.
In the dry seasons of the church, there may be outward signs of
life, but the spiritual hearts of the people have stopped beating.
This does not make the dry seasons any less a part of revival. God
is still sovereign; He is still in charge. The dryness is just as much
a part of the awakening as the prayers themselves. What other
markers of revival can we trace? What other signs of revival mark
our way? Here are just a few.

THE PRINCIPLE OF FULLNESS OF TIME

As it continues in all its "fullness," dryness always leads to desperation. Out of a profound sense of dissatisfaction, often with a certain degree of gloom, people begin to cry out to God. Remember the story of the Hebrides Islands in the late 1940s? A small group of men meeting in a barn began to cry out, "Oh, God, move on your people." Two women, down the road in a neighboring village, began to pray, "Oh, God, move." They cried out because there was nowhere else to turn. Their dryness led to desperation.

The story of the Hebrides is the story of virtually every revival: Out of a remnant, a large-scale movement is born, a movement that encompasses a large area. And often, strangely enough, the spiritual phenomenon that unfolds is largely unknown! Regardless of how anonymous God's hand is, revival occurs in "the fullness of time." His people, in His time, live out a principle of patience and faith in which the longings of God's followers are fully expressed.

PRAY and Experience Scripture

O Lord, I pray, open his eyes that he may see. (2 Kings 6:17, NASB)

Pause now and pray the powerful prayer of Elisha.

Lord, I pray, open the eyes of Your servants that they may see that those who are with us are more than those who are with them. Lord, open my eyes to a remnant of people who are asking You for revival and awakening in spite of the "dryness" of our time. Lord, by Your Spirit, please give me the diligence to persevere in prayer. Encourage my hope for awakening through the prevailing prayers of others.

THE PRINCIPLE OF LEADERSHIP

In any revival, at least one prophet always emerges. Though he or she may be a leader, the person does not "lead" revival in the classic sense of taking control and directing followers to do certain tasks. The prophet doesn't direct the movement, he or she *embodies* it.

Think of the most humble, dedicated follower of Jesus you know. Who do you know that exhibits a devotion to God, service to others, and obedience to the Word, prayer, and sacrifice? This is the kind of leader whose personality is consistent with the people God chooses to embody spiritual awakening.

Regardless of the leaders' unique personalities, revival is always directed by one person: the Lord Himself. In any spiritual awakening there is always one leader and one leader only—God. Through the Holy Spirit, chosen people embody or epitomize what He is doing for their time.

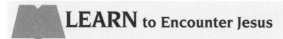

LEARN to Encounter Jesus

I am humble and gentle....(Matthew 11:29)

Pause to meditate on the image of Jesus, who spoke these words. Imagine that Christ stands before you. He has heard your prayers for revival. He has seen your sadness and confusion over the desperate places of our world. Now imagine His response. The Savior doesn't offer you a lecture. He doesn't look at you sternly or with indifference. Instead, the one person who *can* bring revival and who *can* direct our steps toward awakening makes this declaration: "Come to Me. I am here for you as your humble and gentle teacher."

Spend a few moments now, asking for the Spirit's work of Christlikeness in your own life—particularly for His work of humility. Ask the Lord to make this change so that you will be available for all He may desire.

Lord, deepen Your work of humility in me. Just like You, I want to be humble and gentle. I want to be teachable and available. Involve me in Your move of spiritual awakening in whatever ways You desire.

THE PRINCIPLE OF BROKENNESS AND CONFESSION

Brokenness and confession is what the prophet discovers and what the participants in revival experience. When brokenness, confession, and repentance begin to occur among God's people, revival spreads with extraordinary swiftness. As every revival in history bears out, individuals and the church as a whole wake up to the seriousness of their own sin. At times, the remorse can be overwhelming. People become very concerned about the open sins of the flesh and the secret sins of the spirit.

The greatest brokenness occurs in the life of believers as they come to grips with their own lack of love and typically, the result is open and honest confession.

The principle of brokenness and confession yields to a wonderful outcome. As a result of confession and purification of the heart, people become so magnetically attracted to Christ that their dedication grows into a great enthusiasm to follow Him. Naturally, the good news is too life changing, too wonderful to contain. There's an enthusiasm to serve Jesus and a desire to bring others to Him. The person who experiences this new life in God wants everyone to know the One behind this new reality. This is evangelism in its most contagious form.

THE PRINCIPLE OF INFLUENCE

A by-product of evangelism supplies one more principle in the natural development of spiritual awakening. As revival progresses—as the movement of God crests—large numbers of people discover what only a remnant once knew: Jesus Christ is alive! The influence of revival, however, is not limited merely to a spiritual plane. Awakenings have always spilled over beyond the borders of the Church into the life of their towns and cities.

From the time of Hezekiah to the time of John and Charles Wesley in England, revival's influence is always felt in the political and social structure. The Church takes on a new role in society; clergy gain new respect. As revived Christians actually live like Christ, they reach out to their schools, workplaces, and neighborhoods in what some would label "social action." In short, full-fledged revival touches the heart of the whole community.

 SHARE with Others in Community

We loved you so much that we shared with you not only God's Good News but our own lives. (1 Thessalonians 2:8)

Consider praying this prayer with another follower of Jesus. Ask the Lord to empower you to share both your life and the good news with others.

Lord, I ask You to help me share my life with others. Help me convey both my love and Your love. Give us such a passion for sharing our lives and the gospel that a movement begins in our community.

LOVE Others in Community

Ask the Holy Spirit to reveal one specific person who could benefit from your investment of time, of care, and of your life. Who needs the gospel shared through your life?

Lord, show me the person who needs me to share life with them. Who needs Your gospel? Show me, Lord, for I'm listening.

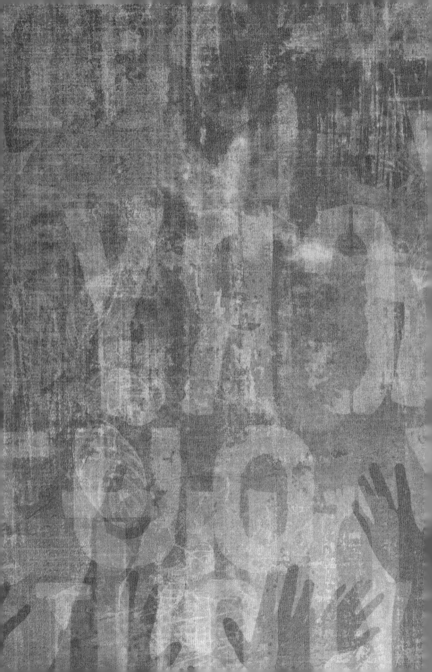

SECTION 4

ENTER BOLDLY INTO BELIEVING PRAYER

*With my voice I cry out to the L*ORD*;*
*with my voice I plead for mercy to the L*ORD*.*
I pour out my complaint before him;
I tell my trouble before him.
(Psalm 142:1–2 ESV)

A SPIRIT-EMPOWERED FAITH

expresses disciplined bold and believing prayer. Let these authors encourage your Spirit-empowered faith:

- Josh McDowell—The Bible: It's All about Relationship
- Ed Stetzer and Philip Nation—Compelled by Love
- Anthony Evans—Turning a Nation to God
- Nick Hall—When We Pray, God Moves

13

THE BIBLE: IT'S ALL ABOUT RELATIONSHIP

From *God Breathed*
by Josh McDowell

CRY OUT TO THE LORD

Lord, I want to know You through the power of Your Word. Give me a renewed perspective of the Bible because I know that it can lead me to a closer relationship with You. Bring me back to the original purpose of Your Word; lead me into a deeper connection with You.

PREFACE

The Bible reveals an infinite God who is holy, all-powerful, and all-knowing—and yet He is intensely relational. He longs to interact with each and every one of us in a personal way. That is the nature of relationship; it is all about wanting to connect intimately with another—and to know that person in a real way. As hard as it may be to comprehend, our infinite, relational God has given us His Holy Spirit and the Bible so we can learn to love and live in an intimate relationship with Him.

God offers to give of Himself to us, and He longs for us to give ourselves wholly to Him as children give themselves to a loving father. Let's consider what Paul wrote to Timothy about the purpose of Scripture: "All Scripture is inspired by God and profitable for teaching, for reproof, for correction, for training in righteousness" (2 Timothy 3:16 NASB). Scripture is not only profitable for teaching (right thinking) and for reproof and correction (right acting); it is also profitable for our relationships, that is, "for training in righteousness."

The word *training* is translated from the Greek word paideia—"to bring up," as in to rear or parent a child. This passage suggests that God's Word is designed to parent us.

Think of it this way: What is it that really parents our own children? Is it the directives, instructions, and commands we give them? Those are behavioral guidelines, but they are not what raise our kids. It is not "parenting," as a concept, that brings up children; it is the parents themselves—relational human beings—who do the work and perform that role. That is the way God designed it. He wants kids to be brought up in loving relationships. Without relationship with another person, all attempts to instill right beliefs and right behavior will be ineffective, because they are detached from the necessary elements of personal love and care.

PRAY and Experience Scripture

All Scripture is inspired by God and is useful to teach us what is true and to make us realize what is wrong in our lives. It corrects us when we are wrong and teaches us to do what is right. (2 Timothy 3:16)

When you hear the benefits of being "parented" by God's Word, how does that touch your heart? Take a moment and read the psalmist's declarations and requests in Psalm 119:11–20. Reflect upon each verse of Scripture. Listen for the Holy Spirit's prompting as He speaks to you about a specific verse that He would like to see become *more* real in your life.

- "I have hidden your word in my heart" (vs. 11).
- "I have recited aloud all the regulations you have given us" (vs. 13).
- "I will study your commandments and reflect on your ways" (vs. 15).
- "I will delight in your decrees and not forget your word" (vs. 16).
- "Don't hide your commands from me!" (vs. 19).
- "I am always overwhelmed with a desire for your regulations" (vs. 20).

Allow the Lord to impress upon you specific ways He would like to use the Word of God to give you instruction, teach you, and parent you.

Lord, I sense that You might want me to experience more of the truth of verse _____. I want to become someone who _____ _____.

The Holy Spirit administers Scripture to us like a loving parent, in order to provide us with wisdom through its lessons (Proverbs 3:5), security through its boundaries (Exodus 20), caution through its warnings (Ephesians 4:17–22), and reproof through its discipline (Philippians 2:3–4). We may study God's Word for correct beliefs. We may even obey God's Word for right behavior. But we must not forget why.

The reordering of my priorities, especially with my wife and children, has been profound due to understanding the relational purpose of God's Word.

Let me take you back to what I did and what I said to Dottie one day when she was hurt by an insensitive parent of another child. It is true that my wife needed to *think* and *act* rightly. And there were plenty of Scriptures available to guide her. But at that particular moment, she needed to *experience* God's Word within the context of a loving relationship with God and with me, her husband.

Because Dottie was hurting, I knew that she needed to experience "the God of all comfort, who comforts us in all our troubles" (2 Corinthians 1:3–4 NIV). At that moment, Dottie didn't need to hear a passage of Scripture about how God is a just judge or how she needed to be patient and kind toward a person who had been unkind to her. What she needed was for her husband to experience *with her* the second half of Romans 12:15: "Weep with those who weep."

So instead of spouting Scripture, I simply put my arms around her and said, "Honey, I am so sorry that you had to hear those words, and I hurt for you."

Dottie felt loved that day when I experienced a simple but profound truth with her from God's book. I also felt a deeper sense of love and meaning from "the God of all comfort," who smiled upon his children as they relationally experienced the truth of his Word.

→ LOVE Others in Community

Weep with those who weep. (Romans 12:15)

Pray for the Spirit's direction and power to care for a family member, coworker, or friend as you complete the sentence below. Is there someone in your life who is experiencing emotional pain, disappointment, or discouragement? You're called to love this person by mourning together or hurting with them. Whom do you know is going through difficult circumstances? I *need to hurt with* _____ *concerning* _____. (For example, I *need to hurt with Kathy concerning her financial stress.*)

Make plans to practice this skill in person.

Then share how it makes you *feel* to hear this person's struggle, life stress, or need for support: I *want you to know that I felt* _____ *as I heard you share about* _____. Or, *My heart hurt when I heard you say* _____. (For example, *Kathy, it hurt my heart when I heard you share about your financial stress. I heard the strain in your voice and could imagine how scary it must be for you. I felt sad when I heard you say that all of this has made it difficult to trust.*)

God gave us the Bible because He wants an intimate loving relationship with us, wants us to enjoy intimate loving relationships with others, and wants our relationships together to extend into eternity. The relational purpose of Scripture is a powerful reality—the amazing truth that God wants you to be in an intimate relationship with Him. Take a moment to allow that truth to sink in. Think of Jesus, through His Holy Spirit, speaking directly to you in very intimate terms. He longs for you to know Him intimately. He longs to fulfill you, complete you, and give you joy as you love Him and love other people. That is why He has given you His Spirit and His Word. Read what He says to you and me:

"You search the Scriptures because you think they give you eternal life. But the Scriptures point to me!" (John 5:39)

"My purpose is to give…a rich and satisfying life." (John 10:10)

"I have told you this so that my joy may be in you and that your joy may be complete. My command is this: Love each other as I have loved you." (John 15:11–12 NIV)

"I pray that they will all be one, just as you and I are one—as you are in me, Father, and I am in you. And may they be in us so that the world will believe you sent me." (John 17:21)

LEARN to Encounter Jesus

Pause quietly and prayerfully receive the words of Jesus, spoken just for you. Now share your heartfelt response.

Thank You, Jesus, that _____.

Allow the Holy Spirit to touch your heart with the truths above. Imagine a few more of Christ's words: *I want you to search the Scriptures and study them carefully, but I want your ultimate destiny to be more intimacy with Me. My Scriptures are meant to guide you, protect you, and bring good things to your life. I gave you My Word so that you can have a rich and satisfying life with Me.*

SHARE with Others in Community

And we are confident that he hears us whenever we ask for anything that pleases him. (1 John 5:14)

Now pray a prayer that you know pleases the Lord and one that He will certainly answer:

God, as You see things about my life that are distracting to my presentation of Christ, I want to be open to You and to others whom You may want to involve in bringing me back to the truth of Your Word. Please send someone into my life who could benefit from receiving some of Your comfort. I want to mourn with someone who is hurting so that I can share the truth of Your Word and point them to You.

14

COMPELLED BY LOVE

From *Compelled: Living the Mission of God*
by Ed Stetzer and Philip Nation

CRY OUT TO THE LORD

*Lord, I cry out to You. Remind me often
of how much You love me so that I can't help
but share that love with others. Compel me to
reach out, extend a hand, and take initiative
to care for others like You care for me.*

PREFACE

The ultimate call on our lives is not measured in success, influence, or status. The standard by which our lives will be measured is how well we love those God has placed in our path. So where do we gain the motivation for this mission? Only when we experience the love of God can we truly begin to understand what is at the center of our calling. It's the love of Christ that compels our mission to love, and it's the love of Christ that will empower it as well.

LUKE 15:1–7, about the one lost sheep, is the first portion of perhaps the most well-known parable in the Gospels. For those who grew up going to church, it conjures up memories of flannel board pictures and spontaneous dramas led by Sunday School teachers. But do not be fooled. It is a story about the very nature of

God and the heart of His church. It is revolutionary—and offensive to many.

In the context of the passage, we hear the Pharisees' words, dripping with sarcasm about Christ's fraternizing with "sinners." They were scandalized by whom He regarded as His friends.

Two thousand years later, we still have that problem. Do we want to do ministry on "that side of town?" Should we really let "those teenagers" go on the retreat? It seems we work hard to insulate ourselves from the very world Jesus says we should be focused on. We have successfully created, without malicious design, a Christian bubble—an evangelical subculture—where Christians live surrounded only by other Christians, and as a result, there are few among the lost whom we get to know intimately.

God's Mission Is Outside the Bubble

Christian experts tell us how to raise our kids, how to handle our finances, what music to buy, what movies to see, and which books to read. The bubble is complete. But God is on a mission outside that bubble.

In God, we find the Father, Son, and Spirit who intentionally search for the lost. God purposely goes to those who are far from Him (that's us). He is fully aware of humankind's fall, yet isn't afraid to get His hands dirty. God seeks the lost, and we—in our missional assignment—are to do the same.

In the Luke 15 parable, the shepherd has 99 of his 100 sheep. I suspect many bosses would be happy if an employee had a 99 percent success rate. If you had a year with 99 percent success, the result would be praise, pay raises, promotions, and recognition at the annual retreat—because, after all, no one can get it right 100 percent of the time. Right?

The Father stands such conventional wisdom on its head. For the Father, if one sheep is lost, He keeps searching "until…" He doesn't give up. His searching is an "until found" search, not "until tired." It is "until rescued," not "until obligations are fulfilled." It is "until redeemed," not "until conscience is alleviated." God's searching love is one that ends in joy. Too often we seek only a sense of relief.

 PRAY and Experience Scripture

So we are Christ's ambassadors; God is making his appeal through us. (2 Corinthians 5:20)

Ask the Holy Spirit to show you what might be hindering you from more effective ministry outside the "Christian bubble." What keeps you from your missional assignments as God's ambassador? Could it be:

- a matter of wrong priorities?
- a struggle with materialism?
- fearful anxiety?
- concerns about receiving others' approval?
- overattention to activity or achievement?
- or preoccupation with your own plans and goals?

Lord, show me what keeps me from becoming more of an ambassador for You.

Quiet your heart and listen until you sense an answer from the Lord. Then complete the sentence: "My ministry as an ambassador for Christ might, at times, be hindered by

_____."

Next, plan to share your response with another person. Then take some time to pray together, asking God to remove these hindrances and empower your change.

LOVE BRINGS BACK THE STRAYS

The Father responds differently when He rescues a stray. He lays the lost lamb across His shoulders. Great care is taken of the lost one. God says, "I will seek the lost, bring back the strays, bandage the injured, and strengthen the weak, but I will destroy the fat and the strong. I will shepherd them justice" (Ezekiel 34:16). It isn't a "get the job done" attitude. Someone is lost—wandering off the path by accident; others are strays—intentionally leaving the path in rebellion. Never minding the reason, the Great Shepherd searches for the lamb, bandages its wounds, and works justly.

When Ezekiel wrote this passage, Israel had been disobeying God's command to care for the poor and oppressed. Selfishness overrode the ethic Yahweh had given them. Ezekiel proclaimed that God is seeking strays—the very sheep that were causing a problem. It's the pet you don't want to chase down the road, the child who continually frustrates you, or the person you see in the mirror every day (because you know your own sin). But God goes searching, even for the most frustrating strays.

 LEARN to Encounter Jesus

The gospel of Mark gives a unique insight into the heart of Jesus. Mark 5 begins by telling of Jairus's request for Christ to heal his dying daughter. Jesus and the disciples begin their journey to the synagogue leader's home, when Mark stops the story. The gospel writer gives pause to tell a second story within the first.

On the way to the "important business" of healing a synagogue leader's daughter, Jesus stops for a woman with an incurable blood disease. Mark helps us notice the contrast between Jesus' response and that of His disciples. Jesus is sensitive to the woman's needs and her desperate demonstration of faith. The disciples, in contrast, seem irritated, frustrated, and downright impatient. Their plans have been interrupted; their "important work" has been thwarted (Mark 5:22–32).

Pause to reflect on Jesus. He's not too busy to stop. He's not too distracted to care. He sees the needs of people others may not see because they are busy with "important business." Tell the Lord about your gratitude.

Lord, thank You for being the kind of God who is not too busy and not too distracted. I'm especially grateful because _____.

Now reflect on your own life. Are you occasionally interrupted by people who need Jesus, just as you are excitedly heading off to do "important" things? Who might be some of these "interrupting" people in your life? Pause quietly in prayer, asking the Lord to make you attentive and to notice those who need Him.

Lord, help me notice and stop for the people around me who might need You. Empower me to show them the same loving compassion that You would show to them if You were physically present with them. Help me not to be so busy with "important things" that I miss what You are doing in my day-to-day life.

LOVE HEALS THE WOUNDED

The Father does not search just so He can be proud of maintaining a 100 percent record. Rather, His searching love is focused on the goal of healing the wounded. When you search for a believer gone astray, you are working alongside God Himself. In the middle of proclaiming the gospel to a lost soul, God is pleading His case through you by His loving heart. As you quietly discuss the claims of Christ with someone "far from God," the Father is planting seed in soil He has already tilled. Even if you give up and leave, He is still at work in that life. The Father's searching love is boundless compared to ours.

Our agenda should change. We have a directive from the Lord to not give up on the people around us. He lovingly and persistently pursues them, and we walk with Him in that pursuit.

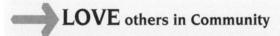 **LOVE** others in Community

Therefore, accept each other just as Christ has accepted you so that God will be given glory. (Romans 15:7)

Take a moment to recall a time when someone looked beyond your faults and saw your needs. When did you receive acceptance in spite of your behavior? Now plan to share this memory with another person. Recount both your experience and your feelings related to the acceptance you received: *Someone looked past my behavior and showed me acceptance when* _____. *And, as a result, I remember feeling so grateful because* _____.

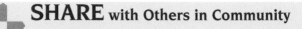# SHARE with Others in Community

Ask the Holy Spirit to give you the opportunity to share some of God's acceptance and care with someone around you.

Lord, show me a person whose behavior is less than perfect, but then give me the opportunity to share some of Your acceptance with them.

Your accepting responses might sound like this: "I know that time must have been so hard for you," or "I am sad that you experienced those difficult things," or "Thanks for telling me about the hard places of your life. We all struggle in some way, don't we?"

15

TURNING A NATION TO GOD

From *America: Turning a Nation to God*
by Tony Evans

CRY OUT TO THE LORD

Lord, I cry out to You because I want to do my part to bring our country back to You. I am depending upon You to change me and reveal Yourself to others through me. Use me for Your glory. Empower me by Your Spirit. Cause my heart to be awakened toward You, and fill me with a passion to serve You.

PREFACE

America is in serious trouble. From sea to shining sea we are witnessing the devolution of a nation. Regardless of which side of the political aisle you sit, it is clear that things are unraveling at warp speed. The United States is quickly becoming the divided states as signs of disunity and conflicts abound. From family breakdowns to the immigration crisis to the abiding racial divide to Congress' inability to function, it is clear we are a fraying nation. Add to this the continuing moral decay that is engulfing us, whether it is the redefinition of marriage and the family, abortions on demand, a media that continues to dumb down decency, or an educational system that increasingly seeks to impart information without ethics in the name of "freedom." We are as a nation sliding south.

But there is a way back. We can return to our roots by a wholehearted pleading of the people of God through repentance and prayer. When we respond in this way, then God will hear our cry, see our hearts, and turn and heal our land.

The American dream is quickly becoming the American nightmare as more and more citizens become disillusioned with the direction things seem to be going. The constant threat of terrorism and an overblown debt threaten not only our economic future, but the future of our children and grandchildren as well. And as people gather unofficially around the water cooler at work—or officially around government-sanctioned summits, seeking to find solutions to the myriad of issues that plague us—real long-term answers continue to elude us.

In the midst of all of this, God's church seems to be of little help in giving real answers to real problems in spite of the proliferation of Christian literature, programming, and facilities. In fact, the Christian faith and its symbols are more marginalized than ever.

There are only two explanations before us as we witness what is happening to our beloved nation. Either we are on the verge of the completion of an eschatology calendar that will usher in the return of Christ to judge the earth and set up His earthly kingdom, or we are enduring the passive wrath of God whereby He allows a person or a society to experience the consequences of their rejection of Him. The more people marginalize the true God of the Bible the more chaotic things become.

However, such judgment opens the door for revival when God's church returns to Him in humility and repentance. The return of Christ is outside of our hands, but revival and its social and cultural benefits are very much in our hands. Even when the church has become an unintentional co-conspirator in the culture's demise through its compromise with the culture, it can be empowered when it turns about to God in repentance.

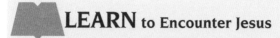

LEARN to Encounter Jesus

Apart from me you can do nothing. (John 15:5)

None of us as individuals, families, or His church has any hope of living an abundant life in our own strength. Take a moment and imagine yourself bowing before the Lord as He reminds you of these things: *Remember, precious child, the air that fills your lungs and every cell of your physical body is a gift that comes from Me. Every thought, plan, strategy, and decision is possible because you are My creation. Your energy, your creativity, your strength, and your intellect are all provisions from Me. You are wonderfully made, but remember that apart from Me you can do absolutely nothing.*

As you bow before the Lord, make a declaration of your helplessness, a declaration of your dependence upon God, and an acknowledgement of your hope in Him.

Lord, my power and strength are insufficient for all that I face in this world—I need You. Restore my perspective. I know I am nothing without You, but I know You are with me, available for me and sufficient for all my needs. I turn to You now.

This is a call for America to turn to God in hopes that He will reverse our course and restore our union to His definition of what a nation is to be when it operates under His rule. *Such a restoration must be led by His church; for God will not skip the church house in order to change the White House* (Ephesians 3:10).

God and His rule is America's only hope; and the church operating under His authority is the means for the realization of that hope, since it alone has been given the keys of the kingdom (Matthew 16:18–19). It is my prayer that God will use this movement to encourage, inspire, and challenge believers in Christ to become kingdom disciples through whom our God can work to bring revival to His church and through it, to our land.

A Declaration of Dependence

Since national revival begins with Christians comprehensively functioning under God's rule, it is past time for a new declaration. America was born out of a desire for independence from the tyranny of England. But spiritual revival demands just the opposite. It requires verbal and visible dependence on God. If we want God to bless America, then America must first bless God. This means His people must first totally dedicate allegiance to Him through the four covenantal kingdom spheres He has established. Those four spheres are personal, familial, the church, and national.

1. **A PERSONAL DECLARATION OF DEPENDENCE**

   Every Christian must decide to no longer serve two masters. God makes it clear that we cannot have the world and have Him at the same time (1 John 2:15–17). Practically this means that God's person, principles, and precepts must be brought to bear on all of our decisions (not just the so-called religious ones). He must be Lord of all of life. Each day must begin with a commitment to Him above all else, and He is to be consulted in prayer on all matters of life (Luke 9:23).

2. **A FAMILY DECLARATION OF DEPENDENCE**

Heads of households must make the declaration of Joshua the slogan for their own home: "As for me and my house, we will serve the Lord" (Joshua 24:15). The dinner table must again become the central place for reviewing and applying kingdom principles (Psalm 128:3). Couples must reconnect themselves to their biblical roles and hate divorce as much as God does (Malachi 2:14). There must be a regular review of the progress the family is making at adhering to godly principles, and the family altar must become central in the home.

 PRAY and Experience Scripture:

So now, come back to your God.

Act with love and justice,

and always depend on him. (Hosea 12:6)

Stop and reflect on your personal relationship with the Lord and your family relationships for a few moments. Ask the Holy Spirit to assess these specific areas of your life. Ask Him to show you if you have strayed from His purposes and His desires and need to return. Declare your dependence upon Him.

God, is there any area of my personal life or family life where I am not allowing You to be Lord? Search me and show me any areas where I have strayed and need to come back to You.

Pause until the Holy Spirit speaks to you. Then make this declaration:

Lord, I declare my dependence upon You. I need Your help to change and I need Your power to act differently, especially in the area of

_____.

3. **THE CHURCHES' DECLARATION OF DEPENDENCE**

Local churches must recommit themselves to their primary responsibility of making disciples and not be satisfied with simply expanding their membership. Jesus doesn't need more fans. He wants more followers. Programs must be evaluated in terms of whether they are growing visible, verbal followers of Christ and not by how many people are entertained by church events. This means that there must be loving accountability incorporated into the life of the church. In addition there must be a radical return by church leadership to the authority of Scripture and priority of prayer as the foundation of church life (1 Timothy 2:8–9). The church must have regular, unified sacred gatherings to keep the focus on our absolute dependency on God.

4. **A NATIONAL DECLARATION OF DEPENDENCE**

The church must again become the conscience of the government. Through its national solemn assembly it should clearly and respectfully call political leaders to God's principles for government (Romans 13:1–7), which means we cannot be so entrenched with political parties that we are not free to speak truth to power. *It also means we must begin speaking with one voice, so the nation sees a unified church and not one divided by faith*. In addition, we should so overwhelm the culture with good works that the benefit we bring cannot be overlooked or denied (Matthew 5:16). Finally, all attempts to remove God from the marketplace ought to be resisted while we simultaneously bring our public officials in prayer before the throne of grace (1 Timothy 2:1–3).

As God's kingdom agenda is manifested simultaneously through His four covenantal spheres, in a spirit of dependence on Him, then we will have done our part in welcoming the glory of our great God to be among us and for God to bring the revival we and our nation so very desperately need, before it's too late.

 # SHARE with Others in Community

Christ in you, the hope of glory. (Colossians 1:27, NASB)

Consider for a moment how God sees you as a bearer of His glory for your family, friends, community, and nation. How does this impact your heart? *When I reflect on the truth that Christ is in me and I get to reveal His glory, I feel*

_____.

Plan to share your reflections with a friend, family member, or small group: *I want to do my part to reveal God's glory—to show the incredible power of Jesus Christ in the world in which I live. He's recently shown me how I need to change* _____ *so that I can be a better representation of Him.*

 # LOVE Others in Community

Ask the Holy Spirit to show you ways in which you can reach out and do your part to overwhelm your community with good works as well. How will you serve the "least of these" in your neighborhood?

→ Holy Spirit, show me how I can "do good" for the people in my community who need it the most. Give me creative ideas and practical applications for how to best love the people You have placed around me. Help me to point others to You as I serve them with the love You have shed abroad in my heart.

16

WHEN WE PRAY, GOD MOVES
by Nick Hall

> ### CRY OUT TO THE LORD
> *Lord, I cry out to You because I want to hear You.*
> *I want to consistently and clearly listen to Your voice*
> *so that I can know You more. Give me a passion for*
> *prayer and an expectancy that when I pray You move*
> *on my behalf. Thank You for giving us the ability to*
> *communicate with you.*

PREFACE

In Ezekiel 3, God tells Ezekiel to speak for Him—to warn the people, both the righteous and unrighteous, about what is about to come. Ezekiel was obedient to the word of the Lord, and he warned the people not to stray away from God. The call was urgent, but what happened next didn't exactly follow a logical action step. Right after calling him to speak to the people, God commanded Ezekiel to go home and *wait* for His command: "Go, shut yourself inside your house" (Ezekiel 3:24).

In the New Testament we see the call to go by waiting. While the Great Commission of Matthew 28 receives the headlines, it was the waiting in Acts 1 that unleashed the power for the cause. So which is it? Are we going or are we waiting? In a task-driven world, it's easy for us to lose the priority of prayer in our drive for "the mission." But Jesus never separated prayer from mission, and He commanded His disciples to follow the same pattern. Only prayer-fueled mission can truly bring spiritual transformation.

MY PERSONAL WAITING GAME

Every year I share the gospel with hundreds of thousands of people. When God first put His call on my life, I couldn't wait to go. But God closed every door until my only ministry was prayer.

During my first semester of college, I studied faith, sought God, and felt the call of an evangelist. Many late nights I would walk into the student chapel where several lights shined on a wooden cross. I would unscrew every light except one, leaving just enough light to see the cross. Then I would cry out to God on my knees, asking Him to use my life to awaken this generation to the reality of Jesus.

Looking back at it now, I understand why that first semester was so important. God was preparing me. He was breaking me. He was slowing me down to show me where true power came from.

PREPARE WITH PRE-PRAYER

A mentor of mine used to say, "We need to prepare our lives with pre-prayer!" We want to be used by God. We want Him to be pleased with the outcome of our lives. But the truth is: God isn't interested in the world *seeing us*; He wants the world to *see Jesus in us*. So we pray. And when we pray, God moves.

I believe we are either prayerful or we are prideful. In the flurry of well-intentioned activity, we lose sight of where our hope is truly found. Prayer is an avenue of surrender. Prayer lays down all of our agendas and says to God Your will be done. Prayer starts on a personal level. Before I can pray, "Jesus, reset this nation," or "Jesus, reset my family," I need to pray, "Jesus, reset me."

Prayer creates intimacy with God and others. God can change our circumstance, but first He wants to change our perspective, to fix our eyes on Him.

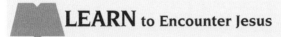

LEARN to Encounter Jesus

Hebrews 3:1 tells us to fix our hearts on the person of Christ: "And so, dear brothers and sisters…think carefully about this Jesus whom we declare to be God's messenger and High Priest." To fix our hearts on Jesus is to relate intimately and lovingly to Him. It will mean focusing our spiritual eyes and the emotions of our heart on the person of Jesus, not just His position. It will mean moving beyond our rational beliefs about the historical Jesus to consider Him and all that He is as the contemporary and very present Jesus.

Fix your eyes on Jesus. Imagine Him sitting on the throne of heaven at the right hand of God. He is the King of kings; the earth is His footstool. Psalm 104:1 tells us that He is robed with honor and majesty. Let the eyes of your heart see the beautiful throne room, His majestic robes, and His royal stature. You see Christ's position and your thoughts align with the beliefs about the Savior, but you have yet to consider the *person of Jesus*.

Imagine Jesus saying these words just to you: I am the One who sits on heaven's throne, but I love to call you My friend (John 15:15). My name is the Most High, the King of all the earth, but you can come to Me any time you desire. I am ready to listen to what you have to say. In fact, I lean in to hear your prayers (Psalm 47:2; 17:6).

I am your Mighty Savior. I am the One who has limitless power and unbridled strength, and yet I can't wait to show you grace. I deeply desire to give you compassion (Isaiah 30:18).

This is the person of Jesus. Consider Him and how He longs to love you, to relate to you. Take the next few moments to relate to Him.

Lord Jesus, when I consider how You are the King of heaven and yet You want to relate to me, my heart is moved with _____. As I fix my eyes on You, I am grateful to You for _____.

Intimacy Creates Boldness

Acts 4 contains one of the boldest prayers from the early church. After being arrested for preaching the Gospel, Peter and John unite the believers—not to gossip or make plans for the best strategy of avoiding government regulations, but to pray. "Now, Lord, consider their threats and enable your servants to speak your word with great boldness" (Acts 4:29).

Boldness doesn't spring up out of nowhere. It comes when we have spent time with Jesus. "When they saw the courage of Peter and John and realized that they were unschooled, ordinary men, they were astonished and they took note that these men had been with Jesus" (Acts 4:13).

I believe that the Holy Spirit is God's anecdote for fear. And God unleashes His Spirit as we meet with Him. Your intimate relationship *with God* results in a bold witness *for God*.

PRAY and Experience Scripture

My purpose is to give [you] a rich and satisfying life. (John 10:10)

Ask God to bring you into such intimacy with Him that a rich, satisfying life and bold witness are the result.

Father God, with a grateful heart I cling to Your promise. Hearing Christ's promise of abundant life gives me security and hope. Open the eyes of my heart so that I can draw closer to You each and every day. I want to see Your plans for bold witness through my life.

SO WHAT DOES THIS ACTUALLY LOOK LIKE IN DAILY LIFE?

One of my favorite encouragements that we use to link prayer and mission is a two-step process called "Keep 5." The idea is simple and reproducible. On an index card or bookmark, write the names of five people in your life who need Jesus. Then take the following steps:

Step 1: Pray

Take five minutes to pray for those five people, that they would know Jesus. Five minutes. Five people. Simple enough!

Step 2: Go

Once we've prayed, we need to put feet to our prayers. The second part of the Keep 5 card is to look for opportunities to share the gospel with those five people. If we pray for opportunities, God gives opportunities! God is often moving all around us—our eyes simply need to be open to it.

If evangelism is hard for you, you're in good company. Sharing your faith isn't supposed to be easy; it's supposed to demonstrate that power belongs to God, not us (2 Corinthians 4:7). Decrease so He can increase.

Although evangelism is hard, the Bible is full of incredible promises to aid those who follow Jesus.

"For the eyes of the Lord range throughout the earth to strengthen those whose hearts are fully committed to Him" (2 Chronicles 16:9).

"We constantly pray for you, that our God may make you worthy of his calling, and that by his power he may bring to fruition your every desire for goodness and your every deed prompted by faith" (2 Thessalonians 1:11).

Prayer and evangelism were never meant to be separated. When we pray, God moves. When God moves, we follow. And when we follow, we will see the Kingdom of God.

 SHARE with Others in Community

Talk to a prayer partner about your encounter with Jesus. Share with him or her about how relating to the person of Jesus is changing your life: *Recently, as I've experienced a deepened intimacy with Jesus,* _____.

→ LOVE Others in Community

So we are Christ's ambassadors; God is making his appeal through us. We speak for Christ when we plead, "Come back to God!" (2 Corinthians 5:20)

Consider how God desires to bless others with His love *through* you. Consider the person of Jesus again and some of

the specific ways He has demonstrated His love to you. Has He provided for you or protected you from harm? Has He accepted you and forgiven you? Has He been attentive to your needs and desires? Has He comforted you and brought you peace?

Now out of your gratitude for receiving His love, become His ambassador. Tell someone this week about one of the ways that Jesus has demonstrated His love to you.

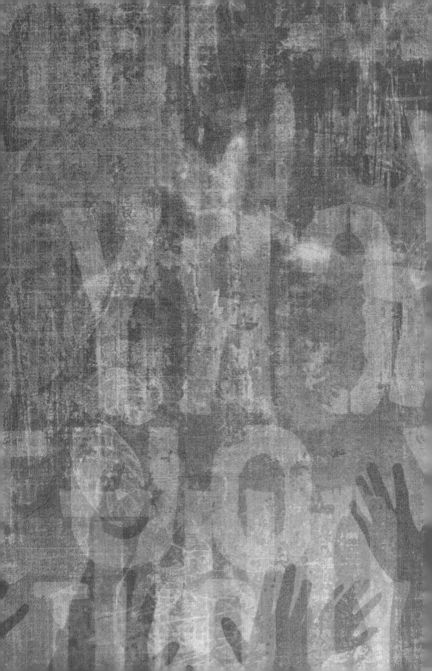

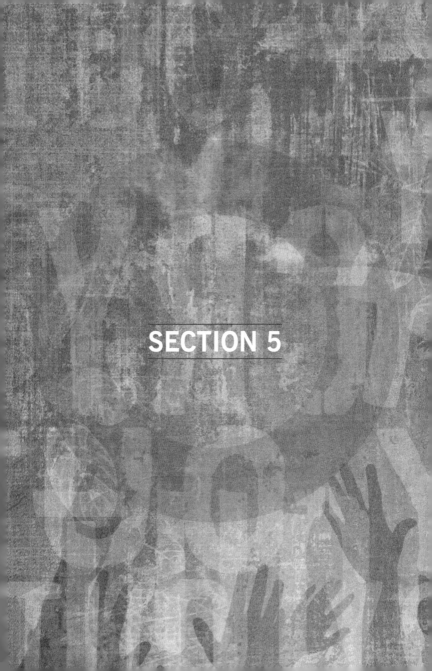

SECTION 5

RECOMMISSIONED FOR THE GREAT COMMISSION

I cry aloud to God,
aloud to God, and he will hear me.
...You are the God who works wonders;
you have made known your might among the peoples.
You with your arm redeemed your people,
the children of Jacob and Joseph.

(Psalm 77:1, 14–15, ESV)

A SPIRIT-EMPOWERED FAITH

champions Jesus as the only hope of eternal life and abundant living. Let these authors encourage your Spirit-empowered faith:

- Alton Garrison—A Spirit-Empowered Disciple
- Oscar Thompson—Concentric Circles of Concern
- Dallas Willard—The Great Omission
- Sammy Rodriguez—Behold the Lamb

17

A SPIRIT-EMPOWERED DISCIPLE

From A *Spirit-Empowered Church: An Acts 2 Ministry Model*
by Alton Garrison

CRY OUT TO THE LORD

*Lord, I cry out to You because I want my life to be
marked by the power of Your Spirit. I want others to
notice in me a relationship with You, Your Word, and
Your people that is different. Empower my witness for
You with the love You have shown to me.*

PREFACE

A Spirit-empowered disciple is one who both lives out the Great
Commandment of loving God and loving people and then is
empowered to fulfill the Great Commission of making disciples.
We know this kind of disciple will never be possible without the
empowerment of the Holy Spirit. And when the Spirit moves, we'll
see a disciple who not only knows the word but lives it out. We'll
see a disciple who has fresh, frequent encounters with Jesus, not
just a one-time salvation experience. And when the Spirit moves
upon the heart of this disciple, there will be a lifestyle of engag-
ing with others in true, vulnerable fellowship. Fulfilling the Great
Commission is a natural outpouring for the Spirit-empowered
disciple.

Our mission, which we call the Great Commission, was established with Christ's words on the Mount of Ascension: "Therefore go and make disciples…" (Matt. 28:19–20 NIV). The Great Commission focuses on the belief system Christ taught, and it establishes the purpose for the church's existence. We are commissioned to worship the Lord with all we have, to win the lost, to train believers to become disciples, to use our ministry gifts, and to find environments of fellowship for connection.

What we often call the Great Commandment serves as a guide for our beliefs—our attitudes and actions—how we go about this Great Commission. Jesus spelled out the Great Commandment, and love was front and center: "'Love the Lord your God with all your heart and with all your soul and with all your mind.' This is the first and greatest commandment. And the second is like it: 'Love your neighbor as yourself'" (Matt. 22:37–39 NIV).

In the light of our mission to make disciples, we can sometimes neglect that love is the guiding force that should govern how we pursue our mission. Paul admonishes us that without love, evidence of Spirit empowerment is hollow and nothing but a clanging cymbal, profiting us nothing. It's as vital to have love guiding our mission as it is to have the Holy Spirit empowering us to complete it.

Our mission is clear. Love is our guide, but what will it look like to make disciples through the lens of love?

THE LIFESTYLE OF DISCIPLESHIP

Spirit-empowered discipleship first requires a lifestyle of fresh encounters with Jesus. We must never get too busy working for Him that we lose our relationship with Him. Paul said, "I count all things to be loss in view of the surpassing value of knowing Christ

Jesus my Lord" (Phil. 3:8 NASB). What kind of encounters with Jesus will mark the Spirit-empowered disciple? Here are just a few:

Jesus longs for our praise—praise from those He has blessed, healed, comforted, and encouraged. Therefore one way to relate to Jesus is to reflect on his divine gifts and then give him praise. He is always comforting, always blessing, always encouraging and always healing, but are we careful to give him praise? Picture him uttering these words: "Where are the (other) nine?" (Luke 17:17 ESV).

Another way to have a productive encounter with Jesus is to be attentive to his voice—listen to him. Many times we think that to love Jesus and relate to him means that we get busy doing things for him. Jesus is actually longing for us to do just what Mary did—give him our undivided, focused attention. Luke wrote, "Mary…sat at the Lord's feet and listened to his teaching" (Luke 10:39 ESV). If we get quiet, we'll hear him speak.

LEARN to Encounter Jesus

That I may know Him and the power of His resurrection and the fellowship of His sufferings….(Philippians 3:10, NASB)

Reflect on the passage mentioned above. Luke 17 describes a painful scene in the life of Jesus. Ten lepers had thrown themselves at the mercy of the Savior and begged Him for healing. Jesus graciously healed each of the ten men, restoring their bodies, and restoring them to their families and their place in the community. But despite this miraculous event, only one of them returned to give Him thanks.

Imagine Jesus, standing on the dusty road, one former leper has bowed before Him to give thanks, and He says, "Where are the (other) nine" (Luke 17:17, ESV)? What does it do to your heart to imagine Christ's disappointment? How does it make you feel to know that the Savior gave these men life, health, restoration, and blessing, and yet only one returned with a grateful heart? Tell Jesus how your heart responds to this incident. Encounter Him; relate to Him because of your love for Him.

Jesus, You would have understandably experienced disappointment and sadness when only one of those men returned to say thanks. It makes my heart sad to know that _____.

Jesus, when I reflect on how You gave the ten men so much and yet they weren't all grateful, I hurt for You because _____.

I don't want to be like the nine lepers who didn't give You thanks. I want to be like the one who returned and thanked You. So please hear my gratitude. Lord, I am grateful today for how You have given me _____.

Secondly, to be a Spirit-empowered disciple, we need frequent experiences of Scriptures. We can't give out what we haven't received. If we love God, we'll love His Word. It's good to know doctrine and even to memorize the Bible, but it's more important to practice the Scriptures daily. That should be our goal.

Peter teaches us, "Since you have in obedience to the truth purified your souls for a sincere love of the brethren, fervently love one another from the heart" (1 Peter 1:22 NASB). Are we practicing that daily? We can practice it by rejoicing with a friend when they have received a great blessing or by comforting a person in their sorrow or by weeping "with those who weep" (Rom. 12:15). This is "doing the Book"!

Anyone who applies the Bible this way is achieving a Spirit-empowered outcome: "Being a living epistle in reverence and awe as His Word becomes real in my life."

 ## PRAY and Experience Scripture

Be happy with those who are happy, and weep with those who weep. (Romans 12:15)

Reflect for a moment on the people around you who have recently experienced a positive event in their lives. Is there someone who's recently had a baby, completed a project, found a job, or completed a class? This person is feeling happy. Romans 12:15 tells us that when others are feeling happy, they need us to join them and express our happiness with them. Here's what expressing happiness might sound like:

- "I am so glad that you _____."
- "I am delighted to hear about your

  _____."
- "I'm excited for you _____."
- "It made me smile to know that you

  _____."

Choose one person who could benefit from your celebration and then plan to "experience Scripture" and do the Book. Celebrate with this person in a note, text, e-mail, or in person.

Finally, a Spirit-empowered lifestyle requires faithful engagement with God's people. We must see people as God sees them or we will never love them as He loves them. We must see people as both fallen and alone. They have spiritual needs as well as relational needs.

My friend, Dr. Ferguson, pointed something out in Scripture that I had never seen before—aloneness actually came before fallenness. In Genesis 2:18, God says that Adam was alone and it was "not good." Several verses before Adam and Eve fell into sin (Gen. 3:6), God declared it was not good that Adam was alone. Ferguson observes, "Ministering acceptance and removing a person's aloneness does not mean that we condone sin. Rather, it means that we look deeper in order to see people's needs."

 SHARE with Others in Community

Reflect on a time when another person looked beyond your sinfulness or fallenness and accepted you anyway. What specific time do you remember someone looking past your faults and meeting one of your needs? Share this story and your gratitude with a friend or prayer partner. Celebrate the faithful engagement of God's people: "I remember a time when someone saw my faults and loved me anyway. I am so grateful for this person because they _____." Or "I am grateful that instead of condemning me or criticizing me, they _____."

I'm convinced that the path to becoming a Spirit-empowered disciple begins with loving God and loving others, which we can't accomplish without the assistance of the Holy Spirit. A clear vision for discipleship means that virtually every church meeting or event must be designed to enhance relationships and equip people to love God with all their hearts, serve God gladly and effectively, and multiply themselves in the lives of others.

→ LOVE Others in Community

One of the best ways to reach people who don't know Jesus is to live out a Bible verse with them rather than quote the verse to them. Think of a person who doesn't know Jesus but who has recently had a positive event occur in his or her life. Live out Romans 12:15 with this person. Be happy when they are happy—rejoice with those who rejoice. You'll be amazed at the connection that's built and the love they will experience as a result of this simple act.

18

CONCENTRIC CIRCLES OF CONCERN

From *Concentric Circles of Concern*
by Oscar Thompson

CRY OUT TO THE LORD

Lord, I cry out to You because I need a renewed passion for those closest to me. I want You to empower me to make disciples in my closest relationships as well as in those I have yet to meet. Help me to ever be reaching out with the life of Christ that You have placed within me.

PREFACE

In the early days of the church, the gospel of Jesus Christ spread through authentic and meaningful relationships. It wasn't through campaigns or creative marketing, advertising or going door to door. The gospel moved in waves of concentric circles, just like the waves created from a rock that's thrown into a pond move out in all directions, rippling further and further out. The gospel is most effective when it begins within our own heart and has its way in our marriage, family, friends, and community—in that order.

If you read through the New Testament, you will see the centrality of relationship. It is nothing profound, but it is just as natural as anything can possibly be. If something is genuine in my life and your life, the natural thing to want to do is to share it with those we know. Relationship: It's the most important word in the English language.

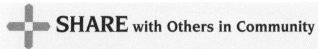

SHARE with Others in Community

Rejoice with those who rejoice. (Romans 12:15, NASB)

Reflect on your own experience of coming to follow Jesus. Can you recall the family members or friends who were there to tell you about the love of Jesus or who shared the gospel with you? Perhaps there was a specific person or group of people who were living examples of Christ's redemption. Reflect on your gratitude for this amazing experience with the Lord.

I feel grateful when I remember how God brought _____ into my life to show me and tell me about Jesus. Without him or her, I don't know where I'd be today.

Share your responses with a prayer partner. Celebrate with one another about God's provision for His people.

EXPERIENCING THE PATTERN

Think of this pattern: Seven concentric circles on a whiteboard. These circles are like a target with a bull's-eye in the center, concentric circles. The circles represent the different relationships of our lives: (1) Self, (2) Family, (3)Relatives, (4) Friends, (5) Neighbors and Associates, (6) Acquaintances, and (7) Person X. The gospel moves on these contiguous lines—on lines of relationship.

I believe that God holds us responsible for everyone he brings into our sphere of influence. Unfortunately, though, many of us who study evangelism seem to go from Circle 1 out to Circle 7 in order to salve our consciences because there are ruptured relationships in Circles 2 through 6 that we prefer to skip over.

When we have ruptured relationships horizontally with people, we also have a ruptured relationship vertically with God. It is not that we do not know the Lord. It is just that he is not really Lord of our lives. We are not willing to let him be Lord of everything. We are not willing to accept, love, and forgive people on his conditions.

With Person X, our lifestyles do not have to be consistent. We can talk to Person X and then be on our way. There is nothing wrong with telling Person X about Jesus. We are supposed to do that. God will bring many strangers into our lives. However, if we cannot tell people in Circles 2 through 6 about the Lord, we are hypocritical. We are play acting. We are unreal people. If our relationship with the Lord is genuine, we will want to share the good news of Christ with those closest to us.

God holds you responsible for every person who comes into your spheres of influence—into your concentric circles. There are people in all of your circles whom you touch every day, and you do not even see them. Some of them are cantankerous; some of them you do not like; and some of them you really do not want to love. But they are there in relationship to you. They are there for you to love—to meet their needs—so the Father can draw them to his Son Jesus.

LEARN to Encounter Jesus

So that you will know what is the hope of His calling, what are the riches of the glory of His inheritance in the saints. (Ephesian 1:18, NASB)

Jesus not only gives you the gift of salvation but He offers you some of His glorious riches too. Christ gives you some of His acceptance, attention, encouragement, comfort, care, support, patience, and kindness. You have received (past tense) Christ's gifts. But now, just as you have received these gifts from Jesus, He asks you to give (present tense) (Matthew 10:8). God's support, care, security, encouragement, patience, kindness, and acceptance are already within you. It is God's desire that you would share these riches with others in your concentric circles.

Jesus, thank You for not only giving me the gift of salvation, but also for filling me with some of Your glorious riches. I'm especially grateful for Your _____.

→ LOVE Others in Community

Do you, at times, feel inconvenienced or even irritated because people in your inner circles actually need you? Take an honest assessment: *When _____ needs _____, I may sometimes feel inconvenienced, interrupted, and irritated.*

Consider what the people in your circles might really need. Could they need God's support shared through you? God's care shared through you? God's kindness shared through you? Or any of His glorious riches listed above? Take a moment to be still before the Lord. Listen to His Spirit as you reflect on the relationships in your circles. Ask Him to reveal the changes that are needed.

Holy Spirit, show me the riches that You have given to me, that are needed in the lives of others. Who needs Your kindness, Your support, Your care, or Your encouragement demonstrated through me today? Speak, Lord, for I am listening.

It seems to me that we are always training people in evangelism to go to Person X out there somewhere. But there is no prior relationship established with Person X. Lifestyle evangelism in the New Testament did not begin with Person X. It worked through relationships that had already been established. Let's look at a few.

ANDREW AND SIMON PETER

At the beginning of his ministry, Jesus began to choose disciples to follow him. Andrew was the first. Notice what Andrew did when he first met Jesus: (John 1:35–42).

When Andrew met the Savior of the world, Jesus the Messiah, his first instinct was to introduce his brother Simon (later named Peter) to Jesus. Though we don't read very much about Andrew, his brother Peter became one of the great leaders of the early church, and he wrote two books of the New Testament. What a contribution Andrew made to the kingdom! He carried the gospel of Jesus Christ to one in his immediate family through a relationship.

PHILIP AND NATHANAEL

Jesus found another disciple from the same hometown as Andrew and Peter: (John 1:43–51).

Philip met Jesus and responded to Jesus' invitation to follow him. He then went to Nathanael and brought his friend to meet Jesus. When Nathanael met Jesus, he acknowledged that Jesus must be the Son of God and the King of Israel. Many believe that Nathanael is the same person who is called Bartholomew in the other three gospels. These two friends became two of the twelve disciples Jesus chose to be his closest companions. Philip carried the good news about Jesus through a relationship to his friend, and both their lives were forever changed.

THE WOMAN AT THE WELL AND HER NEIGHBORS

Jesus took his disciples with him on a journey through Samaria—a place that most Jews avoided because of prejudice. Beside the well at a city named Sycar, Jesus introduced himself to a woman as the Christ (Messiah) and as the "living water." She believed him and went immediately to share the good news with her neighbors: (John 4:28–30, 39–42).

Here was a woman who probably was at the well at noon because she was not accepted by the other women who would normally draw water at the beginning or end of the day. She had been through five husbands and was living with a man she was not married to. When she realized that Jesus was the long-awaited Messiah, she hurried back to town to share the good news with her neighbors and relatives. After only two days with Jesus, many believed in him. One woman touched a whole city for Christ.

 PRAY and Experience Scripture

Imagine that you have encountered Jesus during your daily routine, just like the Samaritan woman at the well. You've made choices that you regret, and there are things about your life that bring you embarrassment or shame. Envision the scene of Jesus approaching you and gently asking for a favor. He engages you in conversation and warmly invites you to get to know Him. He reveals truth to you and about you. Your Savior entrusts you with salvation and offers you to drink of His glorious riches. How do these truths impact your heart? Tell Him.

Now take a moment and consider the manner in which Jesus responded to the woman at the well. Remember how

He acknowledged the woman's sin but treated her with respect, a person with intrinsic value in His eyes. The Father's loving plan is that our encounters with Jesus might lovingly transform us into His image. So take a moment and assess your heart.

- What is your attitude toward sin and sinful people?
- How do you treat those whom you know to be "sinners"?
- Do you treat them like Jesus treated the Samaritan woman?

When I consider my own heart and attitude toward other people, Lord, I realize that I do not always accept others as Christ does. I need to show more _____ (respect, acceptance, support) *to* _____ (name a specific person or group of people).

Finally, make plans to experience James 5:16, confessing your wrong attitudes and responses to another person and then praying together: "Confess your sins to each other and pray for each other so that you may be healed" (James 5:16). Then ask the Holy Spirit to show you how you might accept others just as Jesus does—with love, compassion, and a desire for restoration.

19

THE GREAT OMISSION

From *The Great Omission:*
Reclaiming Jesus' Essential Teachings on Discipleship
by Dallas Willard

CRY OUT TO THE LORD

Lord, I cry out to You because I don't
want to forget or omit the necessity of
becoming more like You.
Show me the ways that I need to change.
Make me more like Jesus so that others
can see You and be drawn to You.

PREFACE

The Great Commission of making disciples gives us our destination, while the Great Commandment of loving the Lord and loving others provides the road map to get there. As we become great lovers of God and lovers of people, that "becoming" will draw others to Jesus. Becoming is the critical ingredient, the one we don't want to omit in our spiritual journey. But it is also the ingredient that is easiest to lose sight of, the one that is often neglected without thinking about it. Discipleship is first about becoming, then from who we have become we will live a life that reflects the life of Christ.

A different model of life was instituted in the Great Commission Jesus left for his people. The first goal he set for the early church was to use his all-encompassing power and authority to make disciples without regard to ethnic distinctions—from all nations (Matthew 28:19). That made clear a world-historical project and set aside his earlier strategic directive to go only to the lost sheep of the house of Israel (Matthew 10:6). Having made disciples, these alone were to be baptized into the name of the Father, and of the Son, and of the Holy Spirit. Given this twofold preparation, they were then to be taught to treasure and keep "all things whatsoever I have commanded you" (Matthew 28:20). The Christian church of the first centuries resulted from following this plan for church growth—a result hard to improve upon.

The kind of life we see in the earliest church is that of a special type of person. All of the assurances and benefits offered to humankind in the gospel evidently presuppose such a life and do not make realistic sense apart from it. The disciple of Jesus is not the deluxe or heavy-duty model of the Christian—especially padded, textured, streamlined, and empowered for the fast lane on the straight and narrow way. He or she stands on the pages of the New Testament as the first level of basic transportation in the kingdom of God.

PRAY and Experience Scripture

I no longer call you slaves, because a master doesn't confide in his slaves. Now you are my friends, since I have told you everything the Father told me. (John 15:15)

Jesus desires a deep friendship with you. He desires to share with you, as His disciple, what He has learned from the Father. You have chosen to follow Him, and He has chosen to share with you, reveal Himself to you, and then communicate the gospel through you.

Pause for a moment to consider this wonderful privilege. The God of the universe wants to reveal Himself to *you*. Because you are His disciple and His friend, Jesus wants to be vulnerable with you. How do you feel as you embrace the truth that Christ wants you to know the things that are on His heart? Respond to the Lord as His friend.

Lord Jesus, as I embrace the wonder of friendship with You, my heart responds with _____.

When I consider that You long to share Your heart with me, I am moved with feelings of _____.

Jesus, because I am so grateful that You want this kind of friendship with me, I am motivated to _____. (For example, *spend more time reading the Bible; listen as well as talk to You in prayer; regularly ask You to reveal Yourself in me, especially when I am having a hard time,* etc.)

DISCIPLESHIP THEN

When Jesus walked among humankind there was a certain simplicity to being his disciple. Primarily it meant to go with him, in an attitude of observation, study, obedience, and imitation. There were no correspondence courses. One knew what to do and what it would cost. Simon Peter exclaimed, "Look, we have left everything and followed you" (Mark 10:28). Family and occupations were deserted for long periods to go with Jesus as he walked from place to place announcing, showing, and explaining the here-and-now governance or action of God. Disciples had to be with him to learn how to do what he did.

Imagine doing that today. How would family members, employers, and co-workers react to such abandonment? Probably they would conclude that we did not much care for them, or even for ourselves. Did not Zebedee think this as he watched his two sons desert the family business to keep company with Jesus (Mark 1:20)? Jesus stated a simple fact: it was the only possible doorway to discipleship.

Discipleship Now

Though costly, discipleship once had a very clear, straightforward meaning. The mechanics are not the same today. We cannot literally be with him in the same way as his first disciples could. But the priorities and intentions—the heart or inner attitudes—of disciples are forever the same. In the heart of a disciple there is a desire, and there is a decision or settled intent. Having come to some understanding of what it means, and thus having "counted up the costs," the disciple of Christ desires above all else to be like him.

The disciple is one who, intent upon becoming Christlike and so dwelling in his faith and practice, systematically and progressively rearranges his affairs to that end. By these decisions and actions, even today, one enrolls in Christ's training, becomes his pupil or disciple. There is no other way. We must keep this in mind should we, as disciples, decide *to make disciples*.

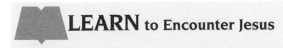

LEARN to Encounter Jesus

The student who is fully trained will be like the teacher. (Luke 6:40)

Imagine Christ standing before you—the only, true Teacher (Matthew 23:10). Listen as He says: "I am the One who *is love* (1 John 4:8). I am the God of all *comfort* (2 Corinthians 1:3–4). I am the One who is *humble and gentle* (Matthew 11:29–30). I am the One who is *moved with compassion* because of the needs of My people (Luke 15:20). I am the One who *encourages* you through Scripture (Romans 15:4). I bear your burdens daily and *support* you in life's struggles (Galatians 6:2)."

Now imagine that the Teacher invites you to become like Him. Jesus asks you to express His love and to extend the light of His presence in a dark world. He invites you to experience His transforming love so that you might be a reflection of His love to those around you.

Pause quietly to consider this question and ask it of the Lord:

Teacher, in what ways do You want me to change? Change me, Lord, because I want to become more like You. Speak, Holy Spirit, for I'm listening.

Wait as the Spirit gives a specific answer and then complete the following sentence: "I sense it would be important for me to become more _____ (comforting, gentle, compassionate, encouraging, supportive, or attentive, etc.) to those in my life."

In contrast, the non-disciple, whether they are inside or outside the church, has something "more important" to do or undertake than to become more like Jesus Christ. An excuse keeps the non-disciple from becoming like Christ and the abundance of life he came to bring. Such lame excuses only reveal that something on that dreary list of security, reputation, wealth, power, sensual indulgence, or mere distraction and numbness, still retains his or her ultimate allegiance.

A mind cluttered by excuses may make a mystery of discipleship, or it may see it as something to be dreaded. But there is no mystery about desiring and intending to be like someone—that is a very common thing. And if we really do intend to be like Christ, that will be obvious to every thoughtful person around us, as well as to ourselves. Of course, attitudes that define the disciple cannot be realized today by leaving family and business to accompany Jesus on his travels about the countryside. But discipleship can be made concrete by actively learning how to love our enemies, bless those who curse us, walk the second mile with an oppressor—in general, living out the gracious inward transformations of faith, hope, and love. Such acts—carried out by the disciplined person with manifest grace, peace, and joy—make discipleship no less tangible and shocking today than were those desertions of long ago.

 # SHARE with Others in Community

No one has ever seen God. But if we love each other, God lives in us, and his love has been brought to full expression through us. (1 John 4:12)

✠ True discipleship, in which we genuinely love God and others, enables the full expression of God's love to be revealed through us. This means that as we experience God's love through the love of other disciples, we see Him as He really is.

How has another follower of Jesus more fully expressed God's love to you? When have you seen another Jesus-follower express or show God's love? Make plans to share words like these: *I've been so impressed by the way you love others, especially how you* _____. *Or I've been able to see a little clearer picture of God because of you.*

➤ LOVE Others in Community

Just as we receive this blessing of experiencing God through other disciples, we are called to express His love to others so they will see God. Ask the Holy Spirit to give insight into how He might want you to more fully express His love in and through you. Does He want you to express His compassion, encouragement, support, acceptance, affection, forgiveness, or mercy to others?

Holy Spirit, who needs me to love them, so that they can see You more clearly? Show me how You want me to love them because I want to be a great expression of You. Speak, Lord, for I am listening. I sense you want me to better express Your love to _____, *especially as I share a portion of Your* _____.

20

BEHOLD THE LAMB

From *The Lamb's Agenda*
by Samuel Rodriquez

CRY OUT TO THE LORD

Lord, I cry out to You. Give me the boldness to declare that You are the Lamb of God who takes away the sins of the world. Empower me to live for You and tell others about who You really are.

PREFACE

The choices we make today will impact our lives tomorrow. The choices we make and how we relate to the Lamb of God determines our destiny in this life and the next. How do you behold the Lamb of God? For how you behold the Lamb will change how you view all of life. When we view the Lamb as the One who sits upon the throne, then we will live our life from that place of authority and power. And because He is on the throne, reigning supreme over all things, He is our hope that all things are going to work out one day.

We have the choice to believe or not believe, to follow a dream or succumb to a nightmare, to lift our heads or walk in sorrow, to stay in the desert or march toward the Promised Land. We have a choice to live by faith or walk by sight, to look back or push forward, to stay silent because of sin or shout for joy because of grace.

This is the choice that Abraham made when he stood determined to climb with his sacrifice, hoping for the lamb:

> Abraham took the wood for the burnt offering and placed it on his son Isaac, and he himself carried the fire and the knife. As the two of them went on together, Isaac spoke up and said to his father Abraham, "Father?" "Yes, my son?" Abraham replied. "The fire and wood are here," Isaac said, "but where is the lamb for the burnt offering?" (Genesis 22:6–7).

WHAT WE CARRY TODAY WILL BE OUR BED FOR TOMORROW

Isaac carried the wood to the very place to which he would be bound in a short while. We should ask ourselves, what are we carrying? The fact is that what we carry up will determine what we bring down. What we carry today will be our bed tomorrow. If we carry bitterness, we will lie on bitterness. If we carry hatred, we will be bound to hatred. If we carry envy, we will lie on envy. But if we carry joy, if we carry peace, if we carry love, if we carry righteousness, we will rest on joy, peace, love, and righteousness in the Holy Ghost. In essence, we will rest in the bounty of the kingdom of God.

PRAY and Experience Scripture

Let us strip off every weight that slows us down, especially the sin that so easily trips us up. (Hebrews 12:1)

Spend a few moments asking the Lord to show you any of the unnecessary things that you are carrying. Is there any weight that needs to be stripped off or any sin that needs to be let go of? Ask the Holy Spirit to examine your life so that you can rest in the bounty of God and then actively engage on mission with Him.

Lord, speak to me about the areas of my life that might be weighing me down? Do I need to strip off bitterness, anger, envy, fear, insecurity, or shame? Do I need to let go of any sins—selfishness, pride, hatred, lust, or greed? Speak to me, Lord.

WHERE IS THE LAMB?

Isaac then asked the $100-million question, "I see the fire, I see the wood, but where is the Lamb?" Sometimes, we find ourselves asking the same question: God, I prayed. I fasted. I confessed, but where is the answer? And just like with Abraham, the answer is that God will provide.

Where is the lamb? For two thousand years humanity asked the same question and then the answer came in John 1:29: "Behold! The Lamb of God who takes away the sin of the world!" (NKJV). Jesus is the Lamb.

Even today, humanity cries out, "Where is the Lamb?" From all strata of society, men and women, children and elders, cry out for the Lamb. Let us rise up and respond with the answer of John the Baptist, "Behold! The Lamb of God." God is now looking for men and women who will not only declare the identity of the Lamb and the provision of the Lamb, but who will hold on to the certainty of the Lamb's agenda so that they desire to do what's right even in the midst of criticism, persecution, and possibly imprisonment or death.

LEARN to Encounter Jesus

Take my yoke upon you. Let me teach you, because I am humble and gentle at heart, and you will find rest for your souls. (Matthew 11:29)

Consider for a moment the invitation of Jesus in Matthew 11. The image He portrays in the text is of Christ standing before us, but He stands in a yoke and the other side of the yoke is empty. The yoke is a tool used long ago to train farm animals. An older animal would take one side of the yoke, while the younger and less experienced animal worked alongside, learning from the experienced one. Imagine that Christ stands before you as the One who is love and invites you to come and take the other side of the yoke.

Imagine now the whispered words of Jesus as the Lord would say to you, "I know there are times when you don't know how to live out My agenda, but you can learn from Me. I can teach you. I know that you may not always understand what it means to live for Me, but I will guide you. I know that there will be times that are hard for you, but rest in the truth that I am bearing the load with you. Would you come and take the other side of this yoke? Together let's live this life well." Pause and respond to His initiation.

Lord Jesus, I am committed to join You and to learn from You. I especially want to join You in _____.

THE LAMB IS ON THE THRONE

Let this generation shake off the shackles of complacency and mediocrity while declaring, "Behold the Lamb! Behold the Lamb who brings forth righteousness and justice. Behold the Lamb who activates sanctification and service. Behold the Lamb who reconciles the message with the march, holiness with humility, and truth with love."

The apostle John saw the Lamb seated on the throne. Not only did the Father provide the Lamb, but he also seated the Lamb on the throne, which means the Lamb rules and governs. As long as the Lamb is on the throne, there is hope.

On a trip to Israel, I visited an olive tree farm. The director of the farm and surrounding campground pointed to an olive tree and asked me to guess the age of the tree. I responded, "One or two hundred years old." She replied, "That tree is somewhere between fifteen hundred and two thousand years old."

I asked, "How can a tree survive that long?" She quickly replied, "That tree has experienced fires and droughts, and it still stands. Simply, the roots are embedded within the rock. As long as the rock does not move, that tree will live."

Christ is our rock. As long as our rock, the Lamb, is on the throne, there is hope for our nation, hope for our children, hope for our faith, and hope for humanity. As long as the Lamb is on the throne, faith, hope, and charity will live.

 SHARE with Others in Community

And the cornerstone is Christ Jesus himself. (Ephesians 2:20)
Meditate on the Lamb of God, who sits on the throne with outstretched arms and nail-pierced hands. He rules the

earth and governs the heavens and yet He welcomes you into His presence and is excited to love you. Because He is both ruler of all and lover of all, we have hope. Make plans to talk to a friend or family member about the hope that you experience when you embrace the truth that Jesus is on His throne as the ruler of all.

Talk also about the hope you feel because you know that Jesus is the God of love and the cornerstone of your faith: "When I rest in the truth that Jesus is on His throne and in charge of our world, it makes a difference in my life because _____." And "When I embrace the truth that Jesus is the God of love and the Father of compassion, it solidifies my faith because _____ _____."

THE LAMB IS OUR HOPE

Revelation 5:5 tells us that it is the Lamb who is capable of opening what others cannot open. And Revelation 5:9 tells us that it is the Lamb who produces a new song. In Revelation 12:11 we learn of the survivors in their battle against Satan, who "triumphed over him by the blood of the Lamb and by the word of their testimony; they did not love their lives so much as to shrink from death."

The Lamb's agenda opens the book and reveals truth. The Lamb's agenda produces a new song, the song of the redeemed. The Lamb's agenda enables us to overcome, for we cannot dance in the Promised Land until we learn to sing in the desert.

Therefore, let us press forward with the agenda of the Lamb. Let us speak to the barrio and Beverly Hills, to those on Wall Street and Main Street, to all in this generation tired of partisan politics, tired of archaic nomenclature, tired of discord and strife, but hungry for righteousness and justice. To you I say, let us stand up and declare, "Behold! The Lamb of God who takes away the sin of all mankind."

> "TO HIM WHO SITS ON THE THRONE AND TO THE LAMB BE PRAISE AND HONOR AND GLORY AND POWER, FOR EVER AND EVER!" (REVELATION 5:13)

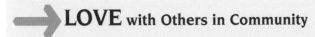

LOVE with Others in Community

Ask the Holy Spirit to prompt you and give you boldness as you declare to others that Jesus is the Lamb of God and that He takes away the sins of the world.

Appendix

ABOUT THE AUTHORS AND THEIR RESOURCES

MARK BATTERSON
Excerpt from: **Wild Goose Chase: Reclaim the Adventure of Pursuing God**
Copyright © 2008 by Mark Batterson
Publisher: WaterBrook Multnomah, an imprint of the Crown Publishing Group
ISBN: 978-1-59052-719-1

ABOUT THE AUTHOR:

Mark Batterson is the *New York Times* best-selling author of *The Circle Maker*, *The Grave Robber*, and *A Trip around the Sun*. He is the lead pastor of National Community Church, one church with seven campuses in Washington, DC. Mark has a doctor of ministry degree from Regent University and lives on Capitol Hill with his wife, Lora, and their three children. Learn more at: www.markbatterson.com.

• • • • •

DOUG BEACHAM
Excerpt from: **Solemn Assembly: Seizing the Future on Our Knees**
General Superintendent's presentation, IPHC National Conference (1996) Solemn Assembly, Northwood Temple, Fayetteville, NC.

ABOUT THE AUTHOR:

A. D. (Doug) Beacham is the General Superintendent and Presiding Bishop of the International Pentecostal Holiness Church. He is an accomplished leader, writer, teacher, and speaker. Before his election as General Superintendent, he served as the executive director of World Missions Ministries. Doug has published six books, the latest of which is *The Christmas Spirit*. In addition to his service within the church, Dr. Beacham represents the IPHC at various organizations and gatherings. For more information, visit: www.iphc.org.

• • • • •

DAVE BUTTS
Excerpt from: **When God Shows Up: Essays on Revival**
Copyright © 2013 by David Butts
Publisher: PrayerShop Publishing
Terre Haute, IN 47801
www.prayershop.org
ISBN: 978-1-935012-46-7

About the Author:

David Butts is President of Harvest Prayer Ministries. He also serves in the following positions: President, Gospel Revivals, Inc. (Herald of His Coming); Chairman, America's National Prayer Committee; Facilitation Committee, Mission America Coalition; Executive Committee, Awakening America Alliance. Besides authoring numerous magazine articles on prayer and missions for various publications, Dave is the author of: *Forgotten Power*; *When God Shows Up: Essays on Revival*; and *Pray Like the King: Lessons from the Prayers of Israel's Kings*, which he wrote jointly with his wife, Kim. To purchase resources: www.prayershop.org. For scheduling, contact: dave@harvestprayer.com.

• • • • •

FRANCES CHAN
Excerpt from: **Forgotten God: Reversing Our Tragic Neglect of the Holy Spirit**
Copyright © 2009 by Francis Chan
Publisher: David C. Cook
ISBN 978-1-4347-6795-0
Default Bible translation: ESV

About the Author:

Francis Chan is the former teaching pastor of Cornerstone Community Church in Simi Valley, CA, a church he and his wife started in 1994. He is also the Founder and Chancellor of Eternity Bible College and author of the best-selling books *Crazy Love: Overwhelmed by a Relentless God*, and most recently, *You and Me Forever: Marriage in Light of Eternity*. For more, visit: francischan.org.

• • • • •

ANTHONY EVANS
Excerpt from: ***America: Turning a Nation to God***
Copyright © 2015 by Anthony T. Evans
Publisher: Moody Publishers
www.moodypublishers.com
ISBN (hardcover): 978-0-8024-1267-6
Default Bible translation: NASB

ABOUT THE AUTHOR:
Tony Evans is one of the most respected leaders in evangelical circles. As a well-known pastor, teacher, author, and speaker, he has devoted his life and ministry to presenting biblical truth and its uncompromising application to the whole of life. Dr. Evans' innate ability to connect biblical principles to everyday realities continues to transform lives all over the world. He has written numerous books and booklets, including *Oneness Embraced*, *The Kingdom Agenda*, *Raising Kingdom Kids*, and *Kingdom Man*. For more information, visit: www.ocbfchurch.org.

•••••

DAVID FERGUSON
Original article by David Ferguson: **"Godly Sorrow: Key to Repentance"**
Contact David at:
2511 South Lakeline Blvd.
Cedar Park, Texas 78713
(512) 795-0498
www.greatcommandment.net

ABOUT THE AUTHOR:
David Ferguson serves as the Executive Director for the Great Commandment Network that serves more than twenty denominations and para-church ministries through pastoral care, training strategies, and resource development. David is a member of the Oxford Society of Scholars and has authored more than twenty-five books, including *Relational Foundations*, *Relational Discipleship*, *Intimate Encounters*, and *The Great Commandment Principle*. David and his wife, Teresa, are the co-founders of Intimate Life Ministries and the Center for Relational Leadership and have conducted training and coaching events for ministers and leaders from more than fifty countries.

•••••

RONNIE FLOYD
Excerpt from: **How to Pray**
Copyright © 1999 by Word Publishing
Publisher: Word Publishing, a Thomas Nelson Company
ISBN: 0-8499-3746-9
Default Bible translation: NASB

About the Author:

Ronnie Floyd was elected president of the Southern Baptist Convention in 2014 and is pastor of Cross Church, a multisite fellowship of believers, in northwest Arkansas. From a desire to influence the vibrant northwest Arkansas business community, he founded the Northwest Arkansas Business Persons Summit. Additionally, he also founded the Cross Church School of Ministry, a one-year ministry residency that prepares leaders for life, ministry, and gospel advancement globally. Currently, he is the general editor of LifeWay's Bible Studies for Life, and author of over twenty books. For more information, visit: www.RonnieFloyd.com. Follow him on Twitter @RonnieFloyd and Instagram@RonnieFloyd.

•••••

DENNIS GALLAHER
Excerpt from e-book: **A Sabbath Rest**
www.amazon.com/dp/B008RLYFL4

About the Author:

Dennis Gallaher and his wife, Jan, have been caring for God's people for thirty-seven years, the past twenty-seven years at Freedom Fellowship Church. They have two grown sons and four grandchildren. Dennis has a degree in Ministry from Hill Country Bible College, a BA in Biblical Counseling from Trinity College, and a MA in Professional Counseling from Texas State University. In their heart of hearts, they are committed to shepherding God's people and loving His church with sincerity and dedication. Read Dennis' blogs at www.dennisgallaher.com and at www.actlikemenblog.com.

•••••

ALTON GARRISON

Excerpt from: **A Spirit-Empowered Church: An Acts 2 Ministry Model**
Copyright © 2015
Publisher: Influence Resources
ISBN: 978-1681540016

ABOUT THE AUTHOR

Alton Garrison serves as the Assistant General Superintendent of the Assemblies of God. In addition, he serves as the director of the Acts 2 Revitalization Initiative, which helps churches renew their spiritual vitality and reach their full kingdom potential. He is the author of *Hope in America's Crisis*; *Building the Winning Team*; *Acts 2 Church*; and *The 360° Disciple*. Garrison and his wife, Johanna, currently reside in Springfield, MO.

•••••

NICK HALL

Original article by Nick Hall: "**When We Pray, God Moves**"
Contact Nick at:
34 13th Ave. NE, Suite B001
Minneapolis, MN 55413
(612) 248-8080
team@pulsemovement.com

ABOUT THE AUTHOR

Nick Hall is the Founder and Chief Communicator for PULSE, a prayer and evangelism movement on mission to empower the church and awaken culture to the reality of Jesus. He sits on the leadership teams for the US Lausanne Committee, the National Association of Evangelicals, the student advisory team for the Billy Graham Evangelistic Association, and the executive committee for Luis Palau's Next Generation Alliance. Nick has a master's in Leadership and Christian Thought from Bethel Seminary in St. Paul, MN. He lives in Minneapolis, MN, with his wife, Tiffany, and son, Truett. They are expecting a baby girl in late 2015.

•••••

KAY HORNER
Original article from Kay Horner: **"A Call to Sacrifice"**
Contact Kay Horner at:
PO Box 3986
Cleveland, TN 37320
(888)-9-AWAKE-US
(888)-929-2538
www.awakeningamerica.us

ABOUT THE AUTHOR:

Kay Horner is the Executive Director of Awakening America Alliance and National Coordinator for the Cry Out America 9/11 Prayer Initiative. The Awakening America Alliance provides a broad umbrella under which the body of Christ can unite together in seeking a contemporary spiritual awakening. Kay makes her home in Cleveland, TN.

•••••

JOSH MCDOWELL
Excerpt from: **God-Breathed: The Undeniable Power and Reliability of Scripture**
Copyright © 2015 by Josh McDowell Ministry
Publisher: Shiloh Run Press, imprint of Barbour Publishing, Inc.
Default Bible translation: NLT

ABOUT THE AUTHOR:

Josh McDowell has been reaching the spiritually skeptical for more than five decades. Since beginning ministry in 1961, Josh has spoken to more than 25 million people in 128 countries. He is the author or coauthor of 148 books, with over 51 million copies distributed worldwide, including Straight Talk with Your Kids About Sex, Experience Your Bible, Evidence for the Historical Jesus, More Than a Carpenter, and The New Evidence That Demands a Verdict, recognized by World Magazine as one of the twentieth century's top-40 books. For additional resources and to reach Josh, visit: www.josh.org.

•••••

BYRON PAULUS AND BILL ELIFF
Excerpt from: **OneCry: A Nationwide Call for Spiritual Awakening**
Copyright © 2014 by Byron Paulus and Bill Eliff
Publisher: Moody Publishers; new edition
ISBN: 13: 978-0802411396
Default Bible translation: NASB

ABOUT THE AUTHORS:

Byron Paulus, as President and Executive Director of Life Action Ministries, oversees numerous revival-oriented outreaches (www.lifeaction.org), including the OneCry movement of believers who are urgently crying out to God to revitalize the church and transform our culture. For more than three decades, Byron has influenced thousands through his various speaking, writing, and leadership endeavors. Byron and his wife, Sue, have raised three children and reside in Niles, MN.

Bill Elliff leads the pastor emphasis of the OneCry movement. As the Senior Teaching Pastor of The Summit Church in North Little Rock, AR, his passion is to see genuine revival and methodological renewal in the church. Bill is a frequent conference speaker, writer, and consultant to churches, drawing from more than forty years of pastoring and revival ministry. He and his wife, Holly, have eight children and live in Little Rock, AR.

•••••

TOM PHILLIPS
Excerpt from: **Revival Signs: The Coming Spiritual Awakening**
Copyright © 1995 by Tom Phillips
Publisher: Vision House Publishing, Inc.
1217 NE Burnside, Suite 403
Gresham, OR 97030
ISBN: 1-885305-15-X
visionpublishinghouse.com

ABOUT THE AUTHOR:

Tom Phillips is the Vice President of the Billy Graham Evangelistic Association. Dr. Phillips is an expert in global evangelism, revival, and church growth and evangelism trends throughout the world. His extensive background of leadership involvements includes leading the training program at the Billy Graham Training Center at The Cove,

Senior Crusade Director (Billy Graham crusades), Director of Counseling and Follow-up (BGEA), School of Evangelism (instructor), and numerous other leadership assignments. For more information, visit: billygrahamlibrary.org.

•••••

SAMUEL RODRIGUEZ

Excerpt from: **The Lamb's Agenda: Why Jesus Is Calling You to a Life of Righteousness and Justice**
Copyright © 2013 by Samuel Rodriguez
Publisher: Thomas Nelson
ISBN: 978-1-4002-0449-6
Default Bible translation: NIV

ABOUT THE AUTHOR:

Rev. Samuel Rodriguez is President of the National Hispanic Christian Leadership Conference, America's largest Hispanic Christian organization. Named by CNN as "The leader of the Hispanic Evangelical Movement" and by the *San Francisco Chronicle* as one of America's new evangelical leaders, Rodriguez is also the recipient of the Martin Luther King Jr. Award presented by the Congress on Racial Equality. A featured speaker in White House and congressional meetings, he has been featured, profiled, and quoted by such media outlets as the *New York Times*, *Christianity Today*, *Washington Post*, *Wall Street Journal*, *Newsweek*, Univision, Fox News, *Time*, and *Ministries Today*. Rodriguez is also the Senior Pastor of New Season Christian Worship Center in Sacramento, CA. For his additional resources or to reach Sammy, contact: www.nhclc.org.

•••••

ED STETZER

Excerpt from the e-book: **Compelled: Living the Mission of God**
Original title: *Compelled by Love*
These excerpts are from the new edition, 2012
Copyright © 2012 by Ed Stetzer and Philip Nation
Publisher: New Hope Publishers
ISBN: 13: 978-1596693517

ABOUT THE AUTHORS:

Ed Stetzer has planted, revitalized, and pastored churches. He has trained pastors and church planters on five continents, holds two master's degrees and two doctorates, and has written dozens of articles and books. Ed is a contributing editor for *Christianity Today*, and a columnist for *Outreach Magazine* and *Catalyst Monthly*, serves on the advisory council of Sermon Central and *Christianity Today's* Building Church Leaders, and is frequently cited or interviewed in news outlets such as USA *Today* and CNN. His primary role is Vice President of Research and Ministry Development for LifeWay Christian Resources.

Philip Nation works as the Director of Adult Ministry Publishing at LifeWay Christian Resources and serves as the teaching pastor for The Fellowship, a multisite church in Nashville, TN. He earned a Doctor of Ministry from Southeastern Baptist Theological Seminary. His books include *Compelled: Living the Mission of God* and *Transformational Discipleship: How People Really Grow*. He is the happy husband to Angie and father to Andrew and Chris.

•••••

JEREMY STORY
Original article by Jeremy Story: **"Transformation Through Prayer and Fasting"**

ABOUT THE AUTHOR:
Jeremy Story has a history of starting great collegiate ministry movements across America. A self-proclaimed "systems man," he seeks to hear from God on how to more effectively reach college students for Christ. Contact Jeremy at (512) 331-5991 or info@campusrenewal.org. Also see Facebook.com/campusrenewal or www.campusrenewal.org.

A Practical Action Point: Apply These Elements to Pray for College Campuses
The Awakening America Alliance is working to build a prayer accord of people praying together in a common rhythm for revival and awakening. Campus Renewal is working with the Awakening America Alliance to mobilize people as part of this rhythm to pray targeted prayers for revival and awakening on college campuses. Colleges are a key place of culture transformation because most of the world's future leader's lifelong worldviews are shaped there.

Join the Campus Renewal Movement prayer accord. Go to: www.campusrenewal.org/awakeningamerica.

•••••

OSCAR THOMPSON

Excerpt from: **Concentric Circles of Concern: Seven Stages for Making Disciples** with Carolyn Thompson Ritzman

Copyright © 1999 by Claude V. King and Carolyn Thompson Ritzmann
Publisher: B & H Publishers
ISBN: 978-0-8054-1959-7
Default Bible translation: NASB

ABOUT THE AUTHOR:

W. Oscar Thompson Jr. was a pastor for twenty years and then took a position as an evangelism instructor at Southwestern Baptist Theological Seminary in Fort Worth, TX. During his time at the seminary, he launched the Oscar Thompson Evangelistic Association and was a consultant for pastors working with the Cancer Counseling and Research Foundation. His life-threatening illness took his life in 1980, and *Concentric Circles of Concern* was released after his death.

•••••

DALLAS WILLARD

Excerpt from: **The Great Omission: Reclaiming Jesus' Essential Teachings on Discipleship**

Copyright © 2006 by Dallas Willard
Publisher: HarperOne; first edition
ISBN: 13: 978-0060882433
Default Bible translation: NIV

ABOUT THE AUTHOR:

Dallas Willard was a Professor in the School of Philosophy at the University of Southern California in Los Angeles. He was Director of the School of Philosophy and taught at the University of Wisconsin. Dallas also lectured and published significant works on the topic of religion. *The Great Omission* received a *Christianity Today* annual Book Award in the Christian Living category in 2007. Another of Dallas' books, *The Divine Conspiracy*, was released in 1998 and selected as *Christianity Today's* "Book of the Year" for 1999.

•••••

MARK WILLIAMS

Excerpt from: **The Praying Church Handbook, Volume II** with P. Douglas Small
Copyright © 2013
Publisher: Alive Publications
www.alivepublications.org
ISBN: 13: 978-0989652520

ABOUT THE AUTHOR:

Mark L. Williams serves as General Overseer for the Church of God, the highest leadership role in the denomination. Elected to the post in 2012, Williams previously served as second assistant general overseer from 2008-2012. Prior to leading the Church of God on the Executive Committee, Williams was state overseer for California-Nevada and was a member of the International Executive Council. He began his ministerial career as an evangelist, traveling on the weekends while earning a degree from Lee University.

O RESET MY WALK WITH GOD

A SPECIAL PRAYER GATHERING OF GOD'S PEOPLE

With humility and repentance, we seek His forgiveness and restoration and commit to re-engage in His divine purpose.

I. Prayers of Humility—*I Choose to Humble Myself and Seek His Face*

O LORD; attend to my cry! Give ear to my prayer from lips free of deceit! I call upon you, for you will answer me, O God; incline your ear to me; hear my words. Wondrously show your steadfast love…Keep me as the apple of your eye; hide me in the shadow of your wings (Psalm 17: 1, 6–8).

We do not know what to do, but our eyes are on you (2 Chronicles 20:12b).

Oh, that we might seek His face. . .not His hand.

If my people, who are called by my name, will humble themselves and pray and seek my face and turn from their wicked ways, then I will hear from heaven, and I will forgive their sin and will heal their land (2 Chronicles 7:14).

II. Prayers of Repentance—*I Will Turn from My Sin and Self-Effort*

Out of the depths I cry to you, O Lord! O Lord, hear my voice! Let your ears be attentive to the voice of my pleas for mercy! If you, O Lord, should mark iniquities, O Lord, who could stand? But with you there is forgiveness, that you may be feared" (Psalm 130: 1–4).

Who may ascend the mountain of the Lord? Who may stand in his holy place? The one who has clean hands and a pure heart (Psalm 24:3–5).

Against you, you only, have I sinned (Psalm 51:4a).

He who conceals his sins does not prosper, but whoever confesses and renounces them finds mercy (Psalm 28:13).Create in me a pure heart, O God, and renew a steadfast spirit within me (Psalm 51:10).

III. Prayers of Yielding—*I Yield to His Lordship and the Spirit's Fullness*

Hear my cry, O God, listen to my prayer; from the end of the earth I call to you when my heart is faint. Lead me to the rock that is higher than I" (Psalm 61:1–2).

"If anyone wishes to come after me, he must deny himself, take up his cross and follow me" (Luke 9:23).

Be filled with the Spirit (Ephesians 5:18).

"He who believes in Me, as the Scripture said, 'From his innermost being will flow rivers of living water'" (John 7:38).

IV. Prayers of Intercession—*Enter Boldly into Believing Prayer*

"With my voice I cry out to the Lord; with my voice I plead for mercy to the Lord. I pour out my complaint before him; I tell my trouble before him" (Psalm 17:1, 6, 8).

". . . THEN will I hear from heaven and heal their land" (2 Chronicles 7:14).

- Restore Our Biblical Foundations
- Restore Our Marriages and Families
- Restore Our Campuses
- Restore Our Communities
- Restore Our Nation

V. Prayers of Recommittment—*Recommissioned for the Great Commission*

I cry aloud to God, aloud to God, and he will hear me. You are the God who works wonders; you have made known your might among the peoples. You with your arm redeemed your people, the children of Jacob and Joseph (Psalm 77 :1, 14–15).

Restore to me the joy of your salvation and grant me a willing spirit to sustain me. THEN will I teach transgressors your ways, and sinners will turn back to you (Psalm 51:12–13).

You will receive power when the Holy Spirit has come upon you and you shall be my witnesses (Acts 1:8).

The harvest is plentiful but the laborers are few; therefore, beseech the Lord of the harvest that He might send out laborers into His harvest (Luke 10:2).

ABOUT THE GREAT COMMANDMENT NETWORK

The Great Commandment Network is an international collaborative network of strategic kingdom leaders from the faith community, marketplace, education and caregiving fields who prioritize the powerful simplicity of the words of Jesus to love God, love others, and see others become His followers (Matthew 22:37-40, Matthew 28:19-20).

THE GREAT COMMANDMENT NETWORK IS SERVED THROUGH THE FOLLOWING:

Relationship Press – This team collaborates, supports, and joins together with churches, denominational partners, and professional associates to develop, print, and produce resources that facilitate ongoing Great Commandment ministry.

The Center for Relational Leadership – Their mission is to teach, train, and mentor both ministry and corporate leaders in Great Commandment principles, seeking to equip leaders with relational skills so they might lead as Jesus led.

The Galatians 6:6 Retreat Ministry – This ministry offers a unique two-day retreat for ministers and their spouses for personal renewal and for reestablishing and affirming ministry and family priorities.

The Center for Relational Care (CRC) – The CRC provides therapy and support to relationships in crisis through an accelerated process of growth and healing, including Relational Care Intensives for couples, families, and singles. www. relationalcare.org

For more information on how you, your church, ministry, denomination, or movement can be served by the Great Commandment Network write or call:

Great Commandment Network
2511 South Lakeline Blvd.
Cedar Park, Texas 78613
#800-881-8008

Or visit our website: www.GreatCommandment.net

A SPIRIT-EMPOWERED FAITH
Expresses Itself in Great Commission Living
Empowered by Great Commandment Love

 begins with the end in mind:
The Great Commission calls us
to make disciples.

"Therefore, go and make disciples of all the nations, baptizing them in
the name of the Father and the Son and the Holy Spirit. Teach these new
disciples to obey all the commands I have given you. And be sure of this:
I am with you always, even to the end of the age." (Matthew 28:19-20)

The ultimate goal of our faith journey is to relate to the person of Jesus, because it is our relational connection to Jesus that will produce Christ-likeness and spiritual growth. This relational perspective of discipleship is required if we hope to have a faith that is marked by the Spirit's power.

Models of discipleship that are based solely upon what we *know* and what we *do* are incomplete, lacking the empowerment of a life of loving and living intimately with Jesus. **A Spirit-empowered faith is relational and impossible to realize apart from a special work of the Spirit.** For example, the Spirit-empowered outcome of "listening to and hearing God" implies relationship—it is both relational in focus and requires the Holy Spirit's power to live.

 begins at the right place:
The Great Commandment calls us to
start with loving God and loving others.

"'You must love the Lord your God with all your heart, all your soul,
and all your mind.' This is the first and greatest commandment.
A second is equally important: 'Love your neighbor as yourself.'
The entire law and all the demands of the prophets are
based on these two commandments." (Matthew 22:37-40)

Relevant discipleship does not begin with doctrines or teaching, parables or stewardship—but with loving the Lord with all your heart, mind, soul, and strength and then loving the people closest to you. Since Matthew 22:37-40 gives us the first and greatest commandment, *a Spirit-empowered faith starts where the Great Commandment tells us to start: A disciple must first learn to deeply love the Lord and to express His love to the "nearest ones"—his or her family, church, and community (and in that order).*[1]

 embraces a relational process of Christlikeness.

Scripture reminds us that there are three sources of light for our journey: Jesus, His Word, and His people. The process of discipleship (or becoming more like Jesus) occurs as we relate intimately with each source of light. [2]

"Walk in the light while you can, so the darkness will not overtake you." (John 12:35)

Spirit-empowered discipleship will require a lifestyle of:
- Fresh encounters with Jesus (John 8:12)
- Frequent experiences of Scripture (Psalm 119:105)
- Faithful engagement with God's people (Matthew 5:14)

 can be defined with observable outcomes using a biblical framework.

The metrics for measuring Spirit-empowered faith or the growth of a disciple comes from Scripture and are organized/framed around four distinct dimensions of a disciple who serves.

Now these are the gifts Christ gave to the church: the apostles, the prophets, the evangelists, and the pastors and teachers. Their responsibility is to equip God's people to do his work and build up the church, the body of Christ. (Ephesians 4:11–12)

A relational framework for organizing Spirit-Empowered Discipleship Outcomes draws from a cluster analysis of several Greek (*diakoneo, leitourgeo, douleuo*) and Hebrew words (*'abad, Sharat*) which elaborate on the Ephesians 4:12 declaration that Christ's followers are to be equipped for works of ministry or service.[3] Therefore, the 40 Spirit-Empowered Faith Outcomes have been identified and organized around:

- Serving/loving the Lord – *While they were* **ministering** *to the Lord and fasting…* (Acts 13:2 NASB).[1]
- Serving/loving the Word – *But we will devote ourselves to prayer and to the* **ministry** *of the word* (Acts 6:4 NASB).[2]
- Serving/loving people – *…through love* **serve** *one another* (Galatians 5:13 NASB).[3]
- Serving/loving His mission – *Now all these things are from God, who reconciled us to Himself through Christ and gave us the* **ministry** *of reconciliation* (2 Corinthians 5:18 NASB).[4]

1 Ferguson, David L. *Great Commandment Principle*. Cedar Park, Texas: Relationship Press, 2013.

2 Ferguson, David L. *Relational Foundations*. Cedar Park, Texas: Relationship Press, 2004.

3 Ferguson, David L. *Relational Discipleship*. Cedar Park, Texas: Relationship Press, 2005.

4 "Spirit Empowered Outcomes," www.empowered21.com, Empowered 21 Global Council, http://empowered21.com/discipleship-materials/.

A SPIRIT-EMPOWERED DISCIPLE LOVES THE LORD THROUGH

L1. Practicing thanksgiving in all things
Enter the gates with thanksgiving (Ps. 100:4). *In everything give thanks* (I Th. 5:18). *As sorrowful, yet always rejoicing* (II Cor. 6:10).

L2. Listening to and hearing God for direction and discernment
Speak, Lord, Your servant is listening (I Sam. 3:8–9). *Mary…listening to the Lord's word, seated at his feet* (Lk.10:38–42). S*hall I not share with Abraham what I am about to do?* (Gen. 18:17). *His anointing teaches you all things* (I Jn. 2:27).

L3. Experiencing God as He really is through deepened intimacy with Him
"Hear, O Israel: The Lord our God, the Lord is one. Love the Lord your God with all your heart and with all your soul and with all your strength" (Deut. 6:4, 5). *Yet the Lord longs to be gracious to you; therefore he will rise up to show you compassion. For the Lord is a God of justice* (Is. 30:18). See also John 14:9.

L4. Rejoicing regularly in my identity as "His Beloved"
And His banner over me is love (Song of Sol. 2:4). *To the praise of the glory of His grace, which He freely bestowed on us in the beloved* (Eph. 1:6). *For the Lord gives to His beloved even in their sleep* (Ps. 127:2).

L5. Living with a passionate longing for purity and to please Him in all things
Who may ascend the hill of the Lord—he who has clean hands and a pure heart (Ps. 24:3, 4). *Beloved, let us cleanse ourselves from all of flesh and spirit, perfecting holiness in the fear of God* (II Cor. 7:1). *I always do the things that are pleasing to Him* (Jn. 8:29). *Though He slay me, yet will I hope in Him* (Job 13:15).

L6. Consistent practice of self-denial, fasting, and solitude rest
He turned and said to Peter, "Get behind me, Satan! You are an obstacle to me. You are thinking not as God does, but as human beings do" (Matt. 16:23). *"But you when you fast…"* (Mt. 6:17). *"Be still and know that I am God"* (Ps. 46:10).

L7. Entering often into Spirit-led praise and worship
Bless the Lord O my soul and all that is within me… (Ps. 103:1). *Worship the Lord with reverence* (Ps. 2:11). *I praise Thee O Father, Lord of heaven and earth…* (Mt. 11:25).

L8. Disciplined, bold and believing prayer
Pray at all times in the Spirit (Eph. 6:18). *Call unto me and I will answer…* (Jer. 33:3). *If you ask according to His will—He hears—and you will have…* (I Jn. 5:14–15).

L9. Yielding to the Spirit's fullness as life in the Spirit brings supernatural intimacy with the Lord, manifestation of divine gifts, and witness of the fruit of the Spirit
For by one Spirit we were all baptized into one body, whether Jews or Greeks, whether slaves or free, and we were all made to drink of one Spirit (I Cor. 12:13). *You shall receive power when the Holy Spirit comes upon you* (Acts 1:8). *But to each one is given the manifestation of the Spirit for the common good* (I Cor. 12:7). See also, I Pet. 4:10, and Rom. 12:6.

L10. Practicing the presence of the Lord, yielding to the Spirit's work of Christlikeness
And we who with unveiled faces all reflect the Lord's glory, are being transformed into His likeness from glory to glory which comes from the Lord, who is the Spirit (II Cor. 3:18). *As the deer pants after the water brooks, so my soul pants after You, O God* (Ps. 42:1).

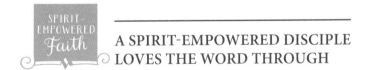

A SPIRIT-EMPOWERED DISCIPLE LOVES THE WORD THROUGH

W1. Frequently being led by the Spirit into deeper love for the One who wrote the Word
"Love the Lord thy God—love thy neighbor; upon these two commandments deepens all the law and prophets" (Mt. 22:37-40). "I delight in Your commands because I love them." (Ps. 119:47). "The ordinances of the Lord are pure—they are more precious than gold—sweeter than honey" (Ps. 19:9-10).

W2. Being a "living epistle" in reverence and awe as His Word becomes real in my life, vocation, and calling

You yourselves are our letter—known and read by all men (II Cor. 3:2). *And the Word became flesh and dwelt among us* (Jn. 1:14). *Husbands love your wives—cleansing her by the washing with water through the Word* (Eph. 5:26). See also Tit. 2:5. *Whatever you do, do your work heartily, as for the Lord…* (Col. 3:23).

W3. Yielding to the scripture's protective cautions and transforming power to bring life change in me

I gain understanding from Your precepts; therefore I hate every wrong path (Ps. 119:104). *Be it done unto me according to Your word* (Lk. 1:38). *How can a young man keep his way pure? By living according to Your word* (Ps. 119:9). See also Col. 3:16–17.

W4. Humbly and vulnerably sharing of the Spirit's transforming work through the Word

I will speak of your statutes before kings and will not be put to shame (Ps. 119:46). *Preach the word; be ready in season and out to shame* (II Tim. 4:2).

W5. Meditating consistently on more and more of the Word hidden in the heart

I have hidden Your Word in my heart that I might not sin against You (Ps. 119:12). *May the words of my mouth and the meditation of my heart be pleasing in Your sight, O Lord, my rock and my redeemer* (Ps. 19:14).

W6. Encountering Jesus in the Word for deepened transformation in Christ-likeness

All of us, gazing with unveiled face on the glory of the Lord, are being transformed into the same image from glory to glory, as from the Lord who is the Spirit (II Cor. 3:18). *If you abide in Me and My words abide in you, ask whatever you wish, and it will be done for you* (Jn. 15:7). See also Lk. 24:32, Ps. 119:136, and II Cor. 1:20.

W7. A life explained as one of "experiencing Scripture"

This is that spoken of by the prophets (Acts 2:16). *My comfort in my suffering is this: Your promise preserves my life* (Ps. 119:50). *My soul is consumed with longing for Your laws at all times* (Ps. 119:20).

W8. Living "naturally supernatural" in all of life as His Spirit makes the written Word (*logos*) the living Word (*rhema*)

Faith comes by hearing and hearing by the word (rhema) *of Christ* (Rom. 10:17). *Your Word is a lamp to my feet and a light for my path* (Ps. 119:105).

W9. Living abundantly "in the present" as His Word brings healing to hurt and anger, guilt, fear, and condemnation—which are *heart hindrances* to life abundant

"The thief comes to steal, kill and destroy…" (Jn 10:10). *I run in the path of Your commands for You have set my heart free* (Ps. 119:32). *And you shall know the truth and the truth shall set you free* (Jn. 8:32). *For freedom Christ set us free; so stand firm and do not submit again to the yoke of slavery* (Gal. 5:1).

W10. Implicit, unwavering trust that His Word will never fail

"The grass withers and the flower fades but the word of God abides forever (Is. 40:8). *So will My word be which goes forth from My mouth, it will not return to me empty"* (Is. 55:11).

A SPIRIT-EMPOWERED DISCIPLE LOVES PEOPLE THROUGH

P1. Living a Spirit-led life of doing good in all of life: relationships and vocation, community and calling

…He went about doing good… (Acts 10:38). *Let your light shine before men in such a way that they may see your good works, and glorify your Father who is in heaven* (Mt. 5:16). *But love your enemies, and do good, and lend, expecting nothing in return, and your reward will be great, and you will be sons of the Most High; for He Himself is kind to ungrateful and evil men* (Lk. 6:35). See also Rom. 15:2.

P2. "Startling people" with loving initiatives to "give first"

"Give, and it will be given to you. They will pour into your lap a good measure—pressed down, shaken together, and running over. For by your standard of measure it will be measured to you in return" (Lk. 6:38). *But Jesus was saying, "Father, forgive them; for they do not know what they are doing."* (Lk. 23:34). See also Lk. 23:43 and Jn. 19:27.

P3. Discerning the relational needs of others with a heart to give of His love

Let no unwholesome word proceed from your mouth, but only such a word as is good for edification according to the need of the moment, so that it will give grace to those who hear (Eph. 4:29). *And my God will supply all your needs according to His riches in glory in Christ Jesus* (Phil. 4:19). See also Lk. 6:30.

P4. Seeing people as needing BOTH redemption from sin AND intimacy in relationships, addressing both human fallen-ness and aloneness

But God demonstrates His own love toward us, in that while we were yet sinners, Christ died for us (Rom. 5:8). *When Jesus came to the place, He looked up and said to him, "Zaccheus, hurry and come down, for today I must stay at your house"* (Lk. 19:5). See also Mk. 8:24 and Gen. 2:18.

P5. Ministering His life and love to our nearest ones at home and with family as well as faithful engagement in His body, the church

You husbands in the same way, live with your wives in an understanding way, as with someone weaker, since she is a woman; and show her honor as a fellow heir of the grace of life, so that your prayers will not be hindered (I Pet. 3:7). See also I Pet. 3:1 and Ps. 127:3.

P6. Expressing the fruit of the Spirit as a lifestyle and identity

But the fruit of the Spirit is love, joy, peace, patience, kindness, goodness, faithfulness, gentleness, self-control… (Gal. 5:22-23). *With the fruit of a man's mouth his stomach will be satisfied; He will be satisfied with the product of his lips* (Prov. 18:20).

P7. Expecting and demonstrating the supernatural as His spiritual gifts are made manifest and His grace is at work by His Spirit

In the power of signs and wonders, in the power of the Spirit; so that from Jerusalem and round about as far as Illyricum I have fully preached the gospel of Christ (Rom. 15:19). *Truly, truly, I say to you, he who believes in Me, the works that I do, he will do also…* (Jn. 14:12). See also I Cor. 14:1.

P8. Taking courageous initiative as a peacemaker, reconciling relationships along life's journey

…Live in peace with one another (I Th. 5:13). *For He Himself is our peace, who made both groups into one and broke down the barrier of the dividing wall* (Eph. 2:14). *Therefore, confess your sins to one another, and pray for one another so that you may be healed* (Jas. 5:16).

P9. Demonstrating His love to an ever growing network of "others" as He continues to challenge us to love "beyond our comfort"
The one who says, "I have come to know Him," and does not keep His commandments, is a liar, and the truth is not in him (I Jn. 2:4). If someone says, "I love God," and hates his brother, he is a liar; for the one who does not love his brother whom he has seen, cannot love God whom he has not seen (I Jn. 4:20).

P10. Humbly acknowledging to the Lord, ourselves, and others that it is Jesus in and through us who is loving others at their point of need
"Take My yoke upon you and learn from Me, for I am gentle and humble in heart, and you will find rest for your souls" (Mt. 11:29). "If I then, the Lord and the Teacher, washed your feet, you also ought to wash one another's feet" (Jn. 13:14).

A SPIRIT-EMPOWERED DISCIPLE LOVES HIS MISSION THROUGH

M1. Imparting the gospel and one's very life in daily activities and relationships, vocation and community
Having so fond an affection for you, we were well-pleased to impart to you not only the gospel of God but also our own lives, because you had become very dear to us (I Th. 2:8-9). See also Eph. 6:19.

M2. Expressing and extending the Kingdom of God as compassion, justice, love, and forgiveness are shared
"I must preach the kingdom of God to the other cities also, for I was sent for this purpose" (Lk. 4:43). "As You sent Me into the world, I also have sent them into the world" (Jn. 17:18). Restore to me the joy of Your salvation and sustain me with a willing spirit. Then I will teach transgressors Your ways, and sinners will be converted to you (Ps. 51:12–13). See also Mic. 6:8.

M3. Championing Jesus as the only hope of eternal life and abundant living
"There is no salvation through anyone else, nor is there any other name under heaven given to the human race by which we are to be saved" (Acts 4:12). "A thief comes only to steal and slaughter and destroy; I came so that they might have life and have it more abundantly" (Jn. 10:10). See also Acts 4:12, Jn. 10:10, and Jn. 14:6.

M4. Yielding to the Spirit's role to convict others as He chooses, resisting expressions of condemnation

"And He, when He comes, will convict the world concerning sin and righteousness and judgment…" (Jn. 16:8). *Who is the one who condemns? Christ Jesus is He who died, yes, rather who was raised, who is at the right hand of God, who also intercedes for us* (Rom. 8:34). See also Rom. 8:1.

M5. Ministering His life and love to the "least of these"

"Then He will answer them, 'Truly I say to you, to the extent that you did not do it to one of the least of these, you did not do it to Me'" (Mt. 25:45). *Pure and undefiled religion in the sight of our God and Father is this: to visit orphans and widows in their distress, and to keep oneself unstained by the world* (Jas. 1:27).

M6. Bearing witness of a confident peace and expectant hope in God's lordship in all things

Now may the Lord of peace Himself continually grant you peace in every circumstance. The Lord be with you all! (II Thess. 3:16). *Let the peace of Christ rule in your hearts, to which indeed you were called in one body; and be thankful* (Col. 3:15). See also Rom. 8:28 and Ps. 146:5.

M7. Faithfully sharing of time, talent, gifts, and resources in furthering His mission

Of this church I was made a minister according to the stewardship from God bestowed on me for your benefit, so that I might fully carry out the preaching of the word of God (Col. 1:25). *"From everyone who has been given much, much will be required; and to whom they entrusted much, of him they will ask all the more"* (Lk. 12:48). See also I Cor. 4:1–2.

M8. Attentive listening to others' *story*, vulnerably sharing of our story, and a sensitive witness of Jesus' story as life's ultimate hope; developing your story of prodigal, pre-occupied and pain-filled living; listening for other's story and sharing Jesus' story

"…But sanctify Christ as Lord in your hearts, always being ready to make a defense to everyone who asks you to give an account for the hope that is in you, yet with gentleness and reverence" (I Pet. 3:15). *"…Because this son of mine was dead, and has come to life again"* (Luke 15:24). See also Mark 5:21–42 and Jn. 9:1–35.

M9. Pouring our life into others, making disciples who in turn make disciples of others

Go therefore and make disciples of all nations, baptizing them in the name of the Father and the Son and the Holy Spirit, teaching them to observe all that I commanded you; and lo, I am with you always, even to the end of the age (Mt. 28:19–20). See also II Tim. 2:2.

M10. Living submissively within His body, the Church as instruction and encouragement, reproof and correction are graciously received by faithful disciples

…And be subject to one another in the fear of Christ (Eph. 5:21). *Brethren, even if anyone is caught in any trespass, you who are spiritual, restore such a one in a spirit of gentleness; each one looking to yourself, so that you too will not be tempted* (Gal. 6:1). See also Gal. 6:2.

May 2016

Listen carefully and you will hear it...the heart-cry for fathers.

Your own heart may be longing for a spiritual father or a mentor. Your children might be missing the loving protection and consistent presence of a dad. You may be burdened by the epidemic of fatherlessness in our generation and your heart aches because of the painful suffering it has produced. What's the answer to these cries of the heart?

Honor your father: when lived out, it's a command that can change the trajectory of generations. It's a command that comes with a promise: honor our fathers (and mothers) and things will go well for us!

Honor Your Father: Reset My Family Legacy tackles challenging topics like:

- How to honor "imperfect fathers."
- Restoring sexual integrity.
- How spiritual fathers (and mothers) can reset a family legacy...in spite of others' failures.
- Becoming a father who is worthy of honor.
- Bringing honor to your children's mother.

Including 80 different exercises designed to help you honor your heavenly Father, pray for your family's legacy, develop a tribute to your Father, and pass on a generational blessing to your children, this resource will equip you to honor your father and reset your family legacy!

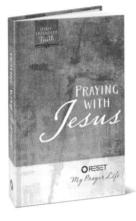
Jesus is praying. Will you pray with Him?

Jesus talks to God on our behalf, but is He praying alone? What would it mean if we joined Jesus in prayer? Praying with Jesus is full of faith-filled prayers to bring hope and new life, along with inspiration and encouragement from leaders and authors:

• Joe Battaglia • Mark Batterson • Jeff Bogue • Dave Butts • Ronnie Floyd • Steve Gaines • Alton Garrison • Steve Hawthorne • Bishop Harry Jackson • Dr. Michael Lewis and Dr. Mark Dance • Josh McDowell • Jedd Medefind • Stormie Omartian and Jack Hayford • Dr. Jared Pingleton • Samuel Rodriguez • Terri Snead • Jeremy Story • Doug Stringer • Dr. Mark L. Williams • George Wood.

Why pray with Jesus? Because as you pray with Jesus, God can supernaturally provide a divine solution for you and divine solution for you and the world He loves. Praying with Jesus will reset your prayer life.

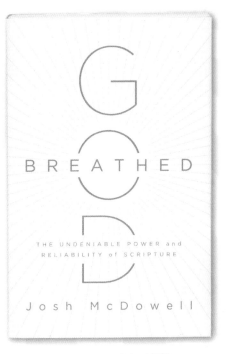

TOGETHER

WASHINGTON, D.C. 7.16.16 NATIONAL MALL

Linking arms, lifting a unified sound asking
Jesus to reset our generation

THE
WORLD
SEES
DIVISION

—

BUT WE CAN CHANGE THAT

JOIN THE CAMPAIGN
RESET2016.COM

@JesusIsTheReset